READING/WRITING
COMPANION

Mc
Graw
Hill
Education

COVER: Nathan Love, Erwin Madrid

mheducation.com/prek-12

Copyright © McGraw-Hill Education

Send all inquiries to:
McGraw-Hill Education
Two Penn Plaza
New York, NY 10121

ISBN: 978-0-07-901829-8
MHID: 0-07-901829-7

Printed in the United States of America.

5 6 7 8 9 LMN 23 22 21 20   B

Welcome to Wonders!

Read exciting **Literature**, **Science**, and **Social Studies** texts!

★ **LEARN** about the world around you!

★ **THINK**, **SPEAK**, and **WRITE** about genres!

★ **COLLABORATE** in discussion and inquiry!

★ **EXPRESS** yourself!

my.mheducation.com
Use your student login to read core texts, practice grammar and spelling, explore research projects and more!

GENRE STUDY **1 REALISTIC FICTION**

GENRE STUDY **2 BIOGRAPHY**

(t) Jeff Mangiat; (b) Library of Congress Prints and Photographs Division [LC-DIG-ppmsca-03128]

GENRE STUDY **3 ARGUMENTATIVE TEXT**

WRAP UP THE UNIT

 Digital Tools Find this eBook and other resources at **my.mheducation.com**

UNIT 4

GENRE STUDY 1 NARRATIVE NONFICTION

GENRE STUDY 2 HISTORICAL FICTION

Anson_iStock/Getty Images

GENRE STUDY 3 NARRATIVE POETRY

WRAP UP THE UNIT

Digital Tools Find this eBook and other resources at **my.mheducation.com**

Talk About It

Volunteering is a way for people to give back to their communities. Look at the photograph. Discuss what the children are doing. In the web below, write some things you could do to help your community. Then talk to a partner about community projects that you would like to make happen.

Helping the Community

Go online to **my.mheducation.com** and read the "Let's Pitch In" Blast. Think about how volunteers can help their communities. Why is volunteering important? Then blast back your response.

TAKE NOTES

Asking questions helps you figure out your purpose for reading. It also lets you think about what you already know about a topic. Before you read, write a question here about Hurricane Katrina.

_____

_____

_____

As you read, make note of:

Interesting Words _____

_____

_____

Key Details _____

_____

_____

_____

_____

_____

REMEMBERING HURRICANE KATRINA

Essential Question

In what ways can you help your community?

Read about how Hector helps others after Hurricane Katrina.

(bkgd) Tyrone Turner/National Geographic/Getty Images; (l)Blend Images/SuperStock; (r) Thomas Barwick/Photodisc/Getty Images; All other images by Jeffrey Mangiat.

Leaning over my steering wheel, I watched the heavy clouds roll in. The sky became a darker shade of gray, and raindrops were soon **scattered** across my windshield. A storm was coming. Glancing at the boxes of clothes stacked in the backseat, I smiled to myself.

A torrential downpour of rain began beating against my windshield as lightning flickered across the sky. I pulled the car off the road until my driving visibility improved. People on the sidewalk held purses and briefcases over their heads in a futile effort to keep from getting wet. Children screamed and danced around in the downpour. The rain reminded me of another storm ten years earlier.

Hurricane Katrina slammed into the Gulf Coast of the United States when I was nine years old. The ferocious storm caused untold amounts of damage.

One of my strongest memories from that time was watching the evening news with my aunt. A reporter stood inside the Houston Astrodome, surrounded by thousands of people. They all shared the same weary expression. Many wore torn and dirty clothes, and some had no shoes on their feet. They slowly shuffled along, their faces full of sadness.

Jeff Mangiat

FIND TEXT EVIDENCE 🔍

Read
Paragraphs 1–2
Point of View

Draw a box around the pronouns in paragraphs 1 and 2 that show who is telling this story. What point of view is the story told in?

Underline the sentence in paragraph 2 that tells you Hector is thinking about an event that happened in the past.

Paragraphs 3–4
Visualize

Circle the words in paragraph 4 that help you picture in your mind the people inside the Astrodome.

Reread
Author's Craft

How does the author show the impact Hurricane Katrina had on Hector?

FIND TEXT EVIDENCE 🔍

Read

Paragraphs 1–3
Point of View

Underline the details in paragraph 3 that tell why Hector is worried that Hurricane Katrina might be a problem for his community.

Paragraphs 4–6
Context Clues

Circle the context clue in paragraph 5 that helps you figure out the meaning of *devised*. Write the meaning below.

_____

_____

_____

Reread

Author's Craft

What can you tell about Hector by the way he acted during Hurricane Katrina?

"Are they here because of the hurricane?" I asked softly.

Aunt Lucia nodded. "*Sí*, Hector. These people are from New Orleans, Louisiana. Just a few days ago, Hurricane Katrina destroyed their homes and possessions, and they lost everything they owned, so now they are temporary **residents** of the Astrodome. It's a place for them to stay until it's safe to go home."

I knew a lot about Katrina. The storm had formed in hot and humid tropical weather and then traveled north. It had come so close to Texas that I worried it would strike us in Houston. It missed us, but other cities were not so lucky.

The TV news reporter looked around. People tried to speak to her, but she was being **selective** about whom she wanted to interview. I noticed a little boy sitting behind her on a cot, hugging an old teddy bear. Watching him, I knew I had to do something.

The next day, my friends joined me at our volunteer club—the Houston Helpers—and together we devised a plan. We wanted to collect toys and give them to the kids at the Astrodome because donating the toys would help bring some happiness into the lives of these families.

Anxious to get started, we made lists of what we needed to do. Then every one of us was **assigned** a specific task.

We agreed to spread the word to our schools and other **organizations**. Three days later, after a Herculean effort on our part, the donation bins were overflowing with new toys!

I'll never forget the day when we entered the Astrodome with our gifts. Children flew toward us from all directions. Smiles lit up their faces as we pulled toys from our bags. Grateful parents thanked us for our **generosity** and complimented our group leaders on how thoughtful and **mature** we all were.

BZZZZ. My cell phone jolted me back to the present, and I noticed that the storm had passed.

"Hector?"

"*Sí*, yes, hi, Jeannie."

"Do you have the donations? A few more families have arrived, more victims of yesterday's tornado."

"Yes, I have the clothing donations. The storm delayed me, but I'll be there soon!"

I **gingerly** eased my car into the suddenly busy traffic. It felt good to know that I was making a difference again.

Summarize

Use your notes to orally summarize the important events in "Remembering Hurricane Katrina."

FIND TEXT EVIDENCE

Read

Paragraphs 1–2
Visualize

Circle the details in paragraph 2 that help you visualize the reactions of the people in the Astrodome.

Paragraphs 3–8
Flashback

What event happens that brings the story back to the present?

_____

_____

Reread

Author's Craft

How did Hurricane Katrina influence what Hector is doing today?

Fluency

With a partner, read aloud the dialogue on page 5. Take turns reading the lines of Hector and his aunt. Say your lines with expression, just as the characters would.

Vocabulary

Use the example sentences to talk with a partner about each word. Then answer the questions.

assigned

The teacher **assigned** the class a book report for next week.

What has a teacher assigned your class recently?

_____

_____

generosity

The children show their **generosity** by collecting food for people in need.

What are some words associated with generosity?

_____

_____

gingerly

I stepped **gingerly** into the cold water of the lake.

What is a reason you might step gingerly?

_____

_____

mature

Mom says I am **mature** enough to babysit my little sister.

What is an antonym for *mature*?

_____

_____

organizations

There are many different **organizations** that help people in need.

What are some organizations that help people in your town or city?

_____

_____

Build Your Word List Pick one of the interesting words you noted on page 2 and look up its meaning in a print or online dictionary. In your writer's notebook, write two sentences using that word: a statement and a question.

residents

The **residents** of our neighborhood had a food drive.

What activities do the residents of your town or city do?

_____

_____

scattered

The papers were **scattered** all over the floor.

What is a synonym for *scattered*?

_____

_____

selective

My father makes healthful meals, so he is **selective** about the food he buys.

What are you selective about?

_____

_____

_____

Context Clues

As you read "Remembering Hurricane Katrina," you may come across a word you don't know. A definition of the word may be in the text nearby, or the word may be restated in a simpler way.

FIND TEXT EVIDENCE

When I read the fifth paragraph on page 4, the phrase collect toys and give them *helps me figure out what the word* donating *means.*

We wanted to collect toys and give them to the kids at the Astrodome because donating the toys would help bring some happiness into the lives of these families.

Your Turn Use context clues to figure out the meanings of the following words.

shuffled, page 3 _____

_____

possessions, page 4 _____

_____

Visualize

As you read "Remembering Hurricane Katrina," visualize the events, characters, and setting in your mind.

FIND TEXT EVIDENCE

On page 3, I can use the details to picture the setting. The narrator describes the rain, the lightning, and the people on the sidewalk holding briefcases and purses over their heads.

Page 3

> Leaning over my steering wheel, I watched the heavy clouds roll in. The sky became a darker shade of gray, and raindrops were soon **scattered** across my windshield. A storm was coming....
>
> A torrential downpour of rain began beating against my windshield as lightning flickered across the sky. I pulled the car off the road until my driving visibility improved. People on the sidewalk held purses and briefcases over their heads in a futile effort to keep from getting wet. Children screamed and danced around in the downpour.

The author describes the sky, the changing weather, and people's actions. I can use these descriptive details to visualize what the setting looks and sounds like.

Your Turn Visualize the scene between Hector and his aunt as they watch the news report. Describe what you "see" to a partner. Remember to use the Visualize strategy.

_____

_____

_____

Flashback

The selection "Remembering Hurricane Katrina" is realistic fiction.

Realistic fiction

- is a made-up story with realistic characters, events, and settings
- includes dialogue
- usually tells story events in sequence
- may include a flashback to an earlier event

Readers to Writers

Writers use flashbacks to help readers better understand a character or situation. By explaining what happened in the past, readers know why characters feel or act the way they do in the present. How can you use flashbacks in your own writing?

FIND TEXT EVIDENCE

I can tell "Remembering Hurricane Katrina" is realistic fiction. The characters, events, and setting could all exist in real life. The story has dialogue and includes a flashback.

Page 3

Leaning over my steering wheel, I watched the heavy clouds roll in. The sky became a darker shade of gray, and raindrops were soon **scattered** across my windshield. A storm was coming. Glancing at the boxes of clothes stacked in the backseat, I smiled to myself.

A torrential downpour of rain began beating against my windshield as lightning flickered across the sky. I pulled the car off the road until my driving visibility improved. People on the sidewalk held purses and briefcases over their heads in a futile effort to keep from getting wet. Children screamed and danced around in the downpour. The rain reminded me of another storm ten years earlier.

Hurricane Katrina slammed into the Gulf Coast of the United States when I was nine years old. The ferocious storm caused untold amounts of damage.

One of my strongest memories from that time was watching the evening news with my aunt. A reporter stood inside the Houston Astrodome, surrounded by thousands of people. They all shared the same weary expression. Many wore torn and dirty clothes, and some had no shoes on their feet. They slowly shuffled along, their faces full of sadness.

Flashback

Sometimes authors do not present a story's events in time order. Authors might take the reader back to an event that happened in the past. This is called a *flashback*.

Your Turn Discuss the beginning, middle, and end of the story. Identify each part as "past" or "present." Write your answer below.

_____

_____

_____

Point of View

The narrator's point of view tells how the narrator feels about characters or events in the story. When the narrator uses the pronouns *I, me,* and *my,* the story is told by a first-person narrator. All the events are seen through the eyes of the narrator.

🔍 FIND TEXT EVIDENCE

On page 3 of "Remembering Hurricane Katrina," the narrator uses the pronouns I, me, *and* my. *That tells me the story is told by a first-person narrator. I can find clues in the text about the narrator's point of view.*

Details
Hector remembers watching the hurricane victims slowly shuffling along with faces full of sadness.
Hector noticed a little boy hugging an old teddy bear and realized he had to do something.

↓

Point of View
The narrator, Hector, thinks it is important to help the hurricane victims.

 Your Turn Reread "Remembering Hurricane Katrina." Find other details that tell Hector's point of view. List them in the graphic organizer on page 11.

Quick Tip

A story told from a first-person point of view uses the pronouns *I, me,* and *my.* A story told from a third-person point of view uses the pronouns *he, she, his,* and *hers.* When a story is told by a first-person narrator, the reader experiences everything the narrator sees, feels, and thinks.

Details

↓

Point of View

Respond to Reading

Discuss the prompt below. Think about how the author tells the order of the events in the story. Use your notes and graphic organizer.

How does the author sequence the events of the story to help you understand how Hurricane Katrina affected Hector?

_____

_____

_____

_____

_____

_____

_____

_____

_____

_____

_____

_____

Quick Tip

Use these sentence starters to discuss the text and organize your ideas.

- *The first part of the story tells about . . .*
- *The middle of the story tells about . . .*
- *The end of the story tells about . . .*

Grammar Connections

As you write your response, remember to use the correct verbs for present and past tenses. For example, in the present tense: *Hector is/makes/wants.* In the past tense: *Hector was/made/wanted.*

Keywords

Keywords are the most important words related to a subject. When you type keywords into a search engine, it sorts through millions of websites that include those words.

- Always use precise, or exact, keywords.
- Use quotation marks around the exact words or phrases that belong together, like a full name or a phrase. The search engine will look for that exact name or phrase.

What keywords would you use to find information about a landmark in your state? Write them here.

_____

COLLABORATE

Make a Public Service Announcement With a partner, research historical landmarks in your state and pick one. You will make a public service announcement (PSA) to convince people to preserve the landmark.

PSAs are short, often 30 seconds or less, so make every word count. Include important facts, such as the answers to these questions.

- Why is the landmark important?
- Why should the landmark be preserved?
- What can people do to help preserve the landmark?

For your PSA, make a video, a slideshow, a podcast, or a poster. In addition to facts, include persuasive language to convince people to preserve the landmark. After you finish, you will be sharing your work.

Aguinaldo

Literature Anthology: pages 178–189

? **How do you know how Marilia feels about going on the field trip?**

Talk About It Reread paragraphs 1–4 on **Literature Anthology** page 183. Turn to your partner and talk about the last thing Marilia has to do.

Cite Text Evidence What clues help you understand what Marilia was feeling about going on the field trip? Write evidence and what it means in the chart.

Make Inferences

When you read about Marilia's actions, what inference can you make about how Marilia will deal with problems she has in the future?

Clue

↓

Clue

↓

Clue

↓

How Marilia Feels

Write I know how Marilia feels about going on the field trip because the author _____

_____

? **How does the author use dialogue to show the relationship between Elenita and Marilia?**

Talk About It Reread the first four paragraphs on **Literature Anthology** page 187. Turn to your partner and discuss what Elenita and Marilia talk about.

Cite Text Evidence What clues help you figure out how they are getting along? Write text evidence in the chart.

Clues	Elenita and Marilia

Write The author uses dialogue to show that Elenita and Marilia are

_____

_____

How does what Marilia tells Margarita on the bus trip back to school help you understand how Marilia feels?

 Talk About It Reread the last three paragraphs on page 188. Turn to your partner and discuss what Margarita and Marilia talk about on the bus.

Cite Text Evidence What does Marilia say that shows how she feels? Write text evidence in the chart.

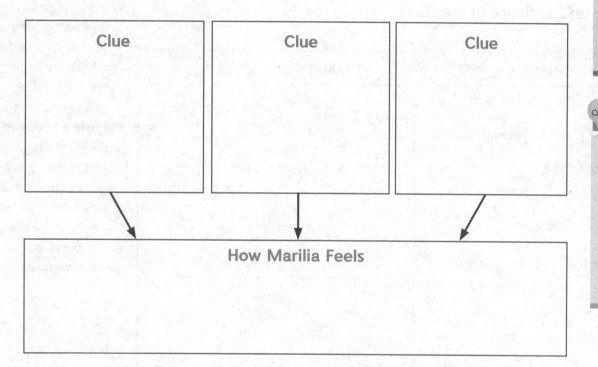

Clue	Clue	Clue

How Marilia Feels

Write The author uses Margarita and Marilia's conversation to help show that _____

_____

_____

Respond to Reading

Discuss the prompt below. Use your knowledge of understanding characters in a story, your notes, and your graphic organizers to help you.

How does the author help you understand how Marilia has changed from the beginning of the story to the end?

_____

_____

_____

_____

_____

_____

_____

_____

_____

_____

_____

_____

Quick Tip

In the beginning of a story, the character may have a problem. By the end of the story, the character may have solved the problem. Use these sentence starters to help organize your text evidence.

- *In the beginning of the story, Marilia's problem is . . .*

- *At the end of the story, Marilia feels better because . . .*

Self-Selected Reading

Choose a text and fill in your writer's notebook with the title, author, and genre of the selection. Record your purpose for reading. Include a personal response to the text in your writer's notebook.

Partaking in Public Service

Literature Anthology:
pages 192–195

There is no doubt about it:

[1] Volunteering is an important part of American life. About 27% of us volunteer in some way. This means that one American out of every four is performing a public service. Many volunteers are teens and children. In fact, in the last 20 years, the number of teen volunteers in this country has doubled. Youth service organizations, such as 4-H clubs, have grown in popularity.

[2] Kids join local volunteer groups to give back to their communities. They work together to help others and to improve their schools and neighborhoods. Community projects may include planting gardens or collecting food and clothing. Some kids raise money for local charities. The volunteer opportunities are limitless.

Reread paragraph 1. **Underline** the clue that tells how the author feels about volunteering. **Circle** two examples in the paragraph that support the author's statement.

Reread paragraph 2 and look at the bar graph. Talk with a partner about how the bar graph helps you understand how kids volunteer.

In the bar graph, **circle** the top volunteer activity for kids. **Draw a box** around the activity that about 21 percent of kids volunteer to do.

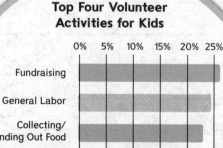

Top Four Volunteer Activities for Kids

| | 0% | 5% | 10% | 15% | 20% | 25% |

Fundraising
General Labor
Collecting/ Handing Out Food
Teaching Younger Kids

3   Alex Lin was just nine years old when he formed the WIN community service team to recycle electronics. By the time he was 16, he had recycled 300,000 pounds of e-waste. He also helped to write a law against e-waste in his home state of Rhode Island.

4   Alex soon realized that reusing was an even better solution to e-waste. Working with his school, he set up a program that fixed old computers and donated them to students in need. Eventually, this program grew. Now it sends computers to people around the world.

5   Erica Fernandez also cares about the environment. She was 16 years old when she heard that a natural gas plant would be built near her hometown. Erica learned that the plant would pollute the air. It would bring harmful chemicals to nearby towns.

6   Erica decided to do something about it. She organized groups to protest the plant. They spoke out publicly. They wrote letters to the government. Eventually, the state agreed to cancel the plans for the plant. Thanks to Erica, the local environment was saved.

Reread paragraphs 3–6. **Underline** text evidence in paragraph 3 that tells what Alex recycles. **Circle** evidence in paragraph 3 that tells how he helped Rhode Island. Then **draw a box** around text evidence in paragraph 4 that tells why he started fixing old computers.

COLLABORATE

Talk with a partner about how Alex's and Erica's projects are both alike and different. **Put checkmarks** in the margin beside the similarities between Alex and Erica and their projects. Write the similarities here.

_____

_____

_____

_____

_____

_____

? **How does the author use what other young people have done to help you see how you can make a difference?**

COLLABORATE

Talk About It Reread paragraphs 3 to 6 on page 19. Talk with a partner about how kids can volunteer.

Cite Text Evidence How does the author help you see that you can make a difference, too? Write text evidence in the chart.

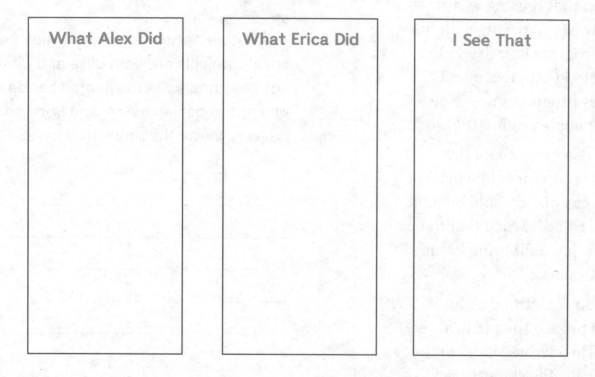

What Alex Did	What Erica Did	I See That

Write The author uses real-life examples of young people who volunteer to _____

_____

_____

_____

Facts and Opinions

A **fact** is something that can be proven to be true. Writers use literal language when presenting facts. Literal language means exactly what it says. An **opinion** is what someone believes to be true. Other people might not agree. Authors use facts and opinions to support an argument. They state a claim—an opinion about a topic. Then they use facts to try to persuade readers to agree.

FIND TEXT EVIDENCE

On page 18 of "Partaking in Public Service," the author begins by giving an opinion: "Volunteering is an important part of American life." The other sentences in the paragraph are facts. The author's purpose in using literal language such as facts is to persuade you to agree with his or her opinion.

Volunteering is an important part of American life. ◄——— **Opinion**
About 27% of us volunteer in some way. This means
that one American out of every four is performing a ◄——— **Facts**
public service.

Your Turn Reread the last paragraph on page 19.

- Which sentence is a fact about what Erica did? _____

  _____

- Which sentence is an opinion? _____

  _____

You can use words or phrases to signal a fact or an opinion. For facts, you can write words such as *in fact, actually,* and *[name of reliable source] says.* For opinions, you can write words such as *in my opinion, I believe, possibly, probably, perhaps,* and *many people think.* Signal words help tell readers whether a detail is a fact or an opinion.

Photodisc/Punchstock

Text Connections

? **How does the artist show a community? How is the artist's idea about community similar to the idea of community in the "Let's Pitch In" Blast, *Aguinaldo,* and "Partaking in Public Service"?**

COLLABORATE

Talk About It Look at the illustration and read the caption. Talk about what you see happening. Discuss how charity events help the community.

Cite Text Evidence **Underline** the people in the illustration who are helping other people. **Circle** the things that tell you where the walk is taking place. Think about how the characters in *Aguinaldo* and the kids in "Partaking in Public Service" help you understand the meaning of community.

Write The artist's idea of community is like the authors' ideas because_____

_____

_____

_____

_____

_____

Twelve community members participating in a charity event in their local park

Present Your Work

COLLABORATE

Discuss how you will present your public service announcement to the class. Use the Presenting Checklist as you practice your presentation. Read your presentation aloud to help you hear any grammatical mistakes. Discuss the sentence starters below and write your answers.

It is important to help preserve state landmarks because _____

_____

_____

I would like to know more about _____

_____

_____

Quick Tip

If you're making a video or movie of your PSA, start by creating a storyboard for your script. A storyboard shows sketches to help the director figure out camera angles and staging. You need an announcer or actor to deliver your PSA message. It takes teamwork and rehearsals to produce a good movie.

✓ Presenting Checklist

☐ Rehearse in front of a friend. Ask for feedback.

☐ Did you speak slowly and clearly, with expression?

☐ Did you get the audience's attention?

☐ Did you cover all the ideas you planned?

☐ Did you give proper contact information to the viewer?

Sean Pavone/Shutterstock.com

Expert Model

Literature Anthology: pages 178–189

Features of Realistic Fiction

Realistic fiction is a form of narrative text. It tells a made-up story that could happen in real life. Realistic fiction

- uses sequence words to tell events in the order they happen

- includes dialogue to develop the plot and characters

- gives sensory details to help readers see, hear, smell, taste, and feel the characters' experiences

Analyze an Expert Model Studying realistic fiction will help you learn how to write a story. **Reread** page 179 of *Aguinaldo* in the **Literature Anthology**. Write your answers below.

How does the nursing home influence the plot? _____

_____

_____

How does the dialogue develop the plot and the main

character, Marilia? _____

_____

_____

_____

Word Wise

On page 181 of *Aguinaldo*, the author uses the Spanish word *hola*, meaning "hello." The author uses other Spanish words throughout the story. By including Spanish words, the author makes the cultural setting of the story more realistic.

Plan: Choose Your Topic

Freewrite With a partner, talk about the times you have felt nervous, such as being on stage or trying a new activity. In your writer's notebook, write all your ideas and thoughts down as quickly as possible. Include as many sensory details as you can. Do not worry about spelling, punctuation, or grammar.

Writing Prompt Choose one of the events from your freewriting. Write a story about a character who is nervous about trying something new.

I will write about _____

Purpose and Audience An author's purpose is his or her main reason for writing. For example, an author writes to inform, or teach; to persuade, or convince; or to entertain.

Think about the purpose for your story. What do you want the reader to think or feel?

My purpose for writing is to _____

Think about the audience for your story. Who will read it?
My audience will be _____

I will use _____ language when I write my story.

Plan In your writer's notebook, use details from your freewriting to make a Sequence of Events Chart. Plot out the main events in your story. What happens first? What event is the climax of your story? What event is the resolution of your story?

Quick Tip

Think about the order of events in your story. Write or draw what happens first, next, and last.

Use these sentence starters.

- *My story will start with . . .*
- *The middle of my story will be about . . .*
- *I will end my story with . . .*

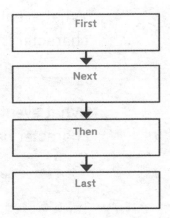

First

↓

Next

↓

Then

↓

Last

Plan: Sequence

What Happens Next? To create a strong story structure, you need to plan the order of events in your story before you begin to write. **Sequence** is the order in which key plot events take place. At the beginning of your story, you introduce your character's problem. In the story's middle, your character works on the problem through one or more events. By the end of the story, your character finds a solution to the problem. To make sure you include everything, answer these questions:

What problem does your character have?

_____

What event happens at the beginning of your story? How is that event the cause of the main character's problem?

_____

What event happens in the middle of your story that shows how the character is working through the problem?

_____

What event happens at the end of your story that shows how the character has solved the problem?

_____

Take Notes Once you know what your story is about, make a list of your settings and characters. Think about how your story will begin. What will make your introduction stronger? Then revise your Sequence of Events Chart to plot out the events of the story.

Draft

Dialogue Authors add dialogue to stories to develop characters and to move the events of the plot along. In the dialogue below from "Remembering Hurricane Katrina," the author uses phrases, such as "lost everything" and "safe to go home," to show that Aunt Lucia is a caring person.

> "Are they here because of the hurricane?" I asked softly.
>
> Aunt Lucia nodded. "*Sí*, Hector. These people are from New Orleans, Louisiana. Just a few days ago, Hurricane Katrina destroyed their homes and possessions, and they lost everything they owned, so now they are temporary **residents** of the Astrodome. It's a place for them to stay until it's safe to go home."

Now use the passage above as a model to write dialogue for a character in your story. What details will your dialogue show about your character?

_____

_____

_____

_____

_____

Write a Draft Use your Sequence of Events Chart to write a draft in your writer's notebook. Remember to write about what the problem is and how it is solved. Use dialogue to show how your characters feel.

Revise

Sensory Details Writers use sensory details to describe the experiences of their characters. Sensory details are words that help the reader see, hear, smell, taste, and feel. Read the paragraph below. Then revise it by adding sensory details. Use a thesaurus to help you find the precise words you need to add sensory details.

Marcy walked past the flowers in the garden. Then a kitten came out of the bushes. The kitten had a collar around its neck, but no tags. Marcy looked into the kitten's eyes and petted her. "Maybe she's lost," Marcy said.

Quick Tip

Adding sensory details will help a reader to visualize the moment. Read this sentence: *I ate a pretzel.*

Now read this revised sentence: *As I crunched down on a handful of pretzel sticks, I tasted salt and butter.*

Which sentence is more interesting? Which one helps you visualize the moment?

Revision Revise your draft, and check that you have sensory details to help your reader see, hear, smell, taste, and feel what the characters do. Check that you have told the story in proper sequence.

Peer Conferences

COLLABORATE

Review a Draft Listen carefully as a partner reads his or her work aloud. Take notes about what you liked and what was difficult to follow. Begin by telling what you liked about the draft. Ask questions that will help the writer think more about the writing. Use these sentence starters.

I enjoyed the beginning of your story because . . .

Can you add dialogue to this scene to show . . . ?

I don't understand the sequence of events when . . . ?

Partner Feedback After your partner gives you feedback on your draft, write one of the suggestions that you will use in your revision.

Based on my partner's feedback, I will _____

_____

_____

After you finish giving each other feedback, reflect on the peer conference. What was helpful? What might you do differently next time?

Revision As you revise your draft, use the Revising Checklist to help you figure out what text you may need to move, elaborate on, or delete. Remember to use the rubric on page 31 to help with your revision.

┌─ **Digital Tools** ─────────────────────────────────┐

For more information on peer conferencing, watch the "Peer Conferencing" video. Go to **my.mheducation.com**.

└───┘

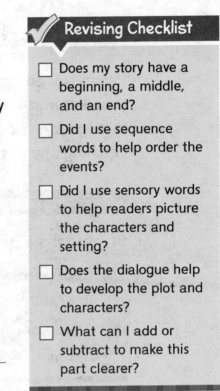

✓ Revising Checklist

☐ Does my story have a beginning, a middle, and an end?

☐ Did I use sequence words to help order the events?

☐ Did I use sensory words to help readers picture the characters and setting?

☐ Does the dialogue help to develop the plot and characters?

☐ What can I add or subtract to make this part clearer?

Edit and Proofread

When you **edit** and **proofread** your writing, you look for and correct mistakes in spelling, punctuation, capitalization, and grammar. Reading through a revised draft multiple times can help you make sure you're catching any errors. Use the checklist below to edit your sentences.

✔ Editing Checklist

☐ Are there action verbs to describe the characters' actions?

☐ Are proper nouns capitalized?

☐ Are quotation marks used correctly in dialogue?

☐ Are possessive nouns and contractions used correctly?

☐ Are all words spelled correctly?

List two mistakes you found as you proofread your story.

1 _____

_____

2 _____

_____

Tech Tip

Spell checkers are useful tools in word-processing programs, but they may not recognize wrong words such as *there* when you mean *they're*. Spell checkers don't replace a careful reading to find errors.

Grammar Connections

When you proofread your essay, you may need to double-check any frequently confused possessives and contractions. You might end up with *its* when you mean *it's, girls* when you mean *girl's*, or *your's* when you mean *yours*.

Publish, Present, and Evaluate

Publishing When you **publish** your writing, you create a neat final copy that is free of mistakes. As you write your final draft, be sure to write legibly in cursive. Check that you are holding your pencil or pen correctly between your forefinger and thumb. Consider adding visuals, such as illustrations or photographs, to help make your story more interesting.

Presentation When you are ready to **present** your work, rehearse reading your story aloud for a friend. Use the Presenting Checklist to help you.

Evaluate After you publish your writing, use the rubric below to **evaluate** your writing.

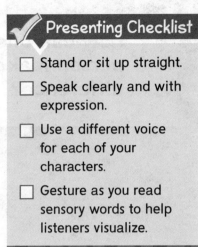

✓ Presenting Checklist

☐ Stand or sit up straight.

☐ Speak clearly and with expression.

☐ Use a different voice for each of your characters.

☐ Gesture as you read sensory words to help listeners visualize.

What did you do successfully? _____

What needs more work? _____

4	3	2	1
• has a clear beginning, middle, and end	• has a beginning, a middle, and an end	• tells a story, sometimes out of sequence	• told in a non-narrative style with no time order
• writing includes rich sensory details	• writing includes some sensory details	• writing includes few sensory details	• writing includes no sensory details
• realistic dialogue develops characters and plot	• dialogue somewhat develops characters and plot	• satisfactory use of dialogue	• very little or unsatisfactory dialogue
• few or no errors in spelling or punctuation	• some errors in spelling and punctuation	• errors in dialogue that might confuse the reader	• many errors make it difficult to follow

Talk About It

Essential Question

How can one person make a difference?

Comic book superheroes are famous for protecting people. However, in real life, it is everyday people who are the real superheroes. They are the ones who help others and who speak out against injustice.

How can you help others? How can you make a difference? Talk to a partner about your ideas. Remember to make eye contact as you speak. Talk at an understandable volume, enunciating and speaking slowly and clearly. Write your ideas in the graphic organizer.

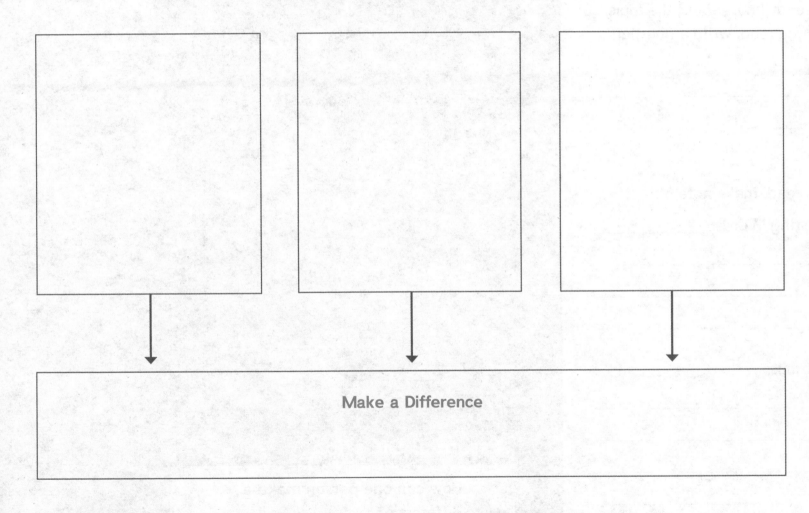

Make a Difference

Go online to **my.mheducation.com** and read the "The Power Is Yours" blast. Think about how an individual can make the world a better place. Blast back your response.

TAKE NOTES

Asking questions will help you figure out your purpose for reading. It also helps you understand what you already know about the topic. Before you read, write a question here.

_____

_____

_____

As you read, make note of:

Interesting Words: _____

_____

_____

_____

Key Details: _____

_____

_____

_____

_____

_____

_____

_____

Judy's APPALACHIA

Essential Question

How can one person make a difference?

Read about how one person decided to take a stand.

Judy Bonds's six-year-old grandson stood in a creek in West Virginia. He held up a handful of dead fish and asked, "What's wrong with these fish?" All around him dead fish floated belly up in the water. That day became a turning point for Judy Bonds. She decided to fight back against the coal mining companies that were poisoning her home.

Marfork, West Virginia

The daughter of a coal miner, Julia "Judy" Bonds was born in Marfork, West Virginia, in 1952. The people of Marfork had been coal miners for generations because coal mining provided people with jobs. Coal gave people the energy they needed to light and warm their homes.

But Marfork wasn't just a place where coal miners lived. Marfork was home to a leafy green valley, or holler, surrounded by the Appalachian Mountains on every side. Judy's family had lived in Marfork for generations. Judy grew up there swimming and fishing in the river. She raised a daughter there.

Mountaintop Removal Mining

An energy company came to Marfork in the 1990s. It began a process called mountaintop removal mining. Using dynamite, the company blew off the tops of mountains to get at the large amounts of coal underneath. The process was quicker than the old method of digging for coal underground, but it caused many problems. Whole forests were destroyed.

Judy Bonds spoke out against mountaintop removal mining.

(b) Bob Bird/AP Images

BIOGRAPHY

FIND TEXT EVIDENCE 🔍

Read

Paragraph 1

Author's Point of View

Underline the detail that tells what Judy's grandson found in a creek. How does the author describe that day as a turning point for Judy Bonds? Write your answer here.

_____

_____

_____

Paragraphs 2-3

Reread

Circle the details in paragraph 2 that tell why coal mining is important to the people of Marfork.

Draw a box around why Marfork is important to Judy.

Reread

Author's Craft

How does the author use a cause-and-effect text structure to organize the information?

FIND TEXT EVIDENCE 🔍

Read

Paragraphs 1–3

Author's Point of View

Underline the effects that mountaintop removal mining had on the people and the land in paragraph 2. How does the author describe Judy's reaction to the pollution? Write your answer here.

_____

_____

Synonyms and Antonyms

Circle the seventh sentence in paragraph 2. Which two words in the sentence are antonyms? Write the two antonyms below. Then write a synonym for each word.

_____

Reread

Author's Craft

What inferences can you make about Judy? Use text evidence.

Dust from the explosions filled the air and settled over the towns. Coal sludge, a mixture of mud, chemicals, and coal dust, got into the creeks and rivers.

Pollution from the mountaintop removal mining began making people living in the towns below the mountains sick. In the area where Judy lived, coal sludge flowed into the rivers and streams. People packed up and left. Judy was heartbroken. The land she loved was being **mistreated**. She realized that the valley that had always been her home had been poisoned. No longer a safe place to live, it had become dangerous. Judy, her daughter, and her grandson had to leave.

Working for Change

Something had to be done about the pollution. Judy decided it was important to **protest** against strip mining and demand that it be stopped. She felt that she must try to keep the area safe for people. She felt **qualified** to talk to groups about the **injustice** of whole towns being forced to move and mountains and forests being destroyed, all because of strip mining. After all, she had grown up in a mining family.

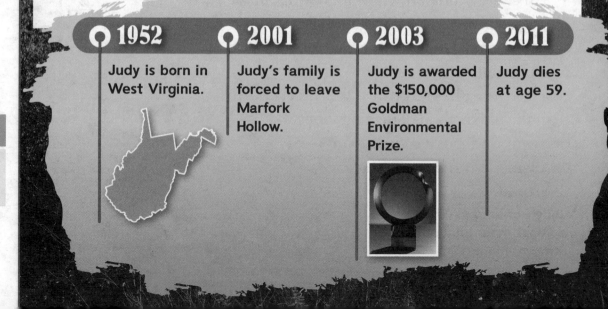

1952	**2001**	**2003**	**2011**
Judy is born in West Virginia.	Judy's family is forced to leave Marfork Hollow.	Judy is awarded the $150,000 Goldman Environmental Prize.	Judy dies at age 59.

Judy worked as a volunteer for the Coal River Mountain Watch, a group that fought against mountaintop removal mining. Eventually, she became its executive director. She **registered** to take part in protests against mining companies. At the protests, Judy faced a lot of anger and insults. Many coal miners were not opposed to mountaintop removal mining. They supported it because they needed the jobs to provide for their families. Judy knew it would be impossible to **boycott** the mining companies. The coal miners could not afford to leave their jobs. Instead, she pushed for changes to be made to the mining process. Slowly, small changes were made to protect communities in mining areas. In 2003, Judy was awarded the Goldman Environmental Prize for her efforts as an activist.

Remembering Judy

Sadly, Judy could not **fulfill** all of her goals. She was diagnosed with cancer and died in January 2011. But her success has provided **encouragement** to other activists. Judy may not have been able to stay in her home, but her work will help preserve and protect the Appalachian Mountains and help others remain in their homes.

Summarize

Use your notes and the timeline to orally summarize the important events in "Judy's Appalachia."

(bkgd) Aimin Tang/R+/Getty Images. (bc) Courtesy Goldman Environmental Prize. (br) Mark Schmerling

BIOGRAPHY

FIND TEXT EVIDENCE

Paragraph 1
Reread

Draw a box around the reason why many people supported mountaintop removal mining. What kind of change did Judy push for? Write your answer here.

_____

_____

_____

Paragraph 2
Timeline

What information in paragraph 2 is also listed on the timeline?

_____

_____

Reread
Author's Craft

What are some of the words and phrases that the author uses to tell about the work Judy did? What is the author's opinion of Judy's work?

Vocabulary

Use the example sentences to talk with a partner about each word. Then answer the questions.

boycott

Joni bought apples instead of grapes after she joined the grape **boycott.**

What would you choose to boycott?

_____

_____

encouragement

The **encouragement** we needed to win the game came from our fans.

What kind of encouragement do you give others?

_____

_____

fulfill

Jules got to **fulfill** his dream of performing in the school talent show.

What dream would you like to fulfill one day?

_____

_____

injustice

The children felt that it was an **injustice** that they were not allowed on the roller coaster because they were too short.

How are _injustice_ and _justice_ related?

_____

_____

mistreated

Tomas felt that the dog's first owner had hurt and **mistreated** her.

What is an antonym for _mistreated?_

_____

_____

Build Your Word List Reread the first paragraph on page 35. Circle the word _leafy_. Look up the word in a thesaurus. In your writer's notebook, write down words with similar meanings. Then, write a sentence using one of your synonyms.

protest

The children decided to **protest** the cutting down of trees in the forest.

What is a synonym for *protest*?

_____

_____

qualified

Doctor Smith and the nurse are **qualified** to tell what treatment the boy needs.

What would you need to do to be qualified for a spelling bee?

_____

_____

registered

The woman gave her address so that she could be **registered** to vote.

Why is it important to be registered to vote?

_____

_____

Synonyms and Antonyms

Authors may use synonyms and antonyms to help you figure out an unfamiliar word. Synonyms are words with similar meanings. Antonyms have opposite meanings.

🔍 FIND TEXT EVIDENCE

In the text below, the word supported *helps me understand the word* opposed. *I know that* supported *means "was in favor of." This will help me figure out what* opposed *means.*

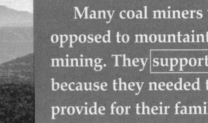

Many coal miners were not opposed to mountaintop removal mining. They supported it because they needed the jobs to provide for their families.

Your Turn With a partner, list synonyms and antonyms for these words from the text:

leafy, page 35 _____

_____

preserve, page 37 _____

_____

Reread

When you read an informational text, you may come across information and facts that are new to you. As you read "Judy's Appalachia," reread sections of text to make sure you understand and remember the information.

🔍 FIND TEXT EVIDENCE

You may not be sure what mountaintop removal mining is. Reread the fourth paragraph of "Judy's Appalachia" on page 35.

Quick Tip

When you reread an informational text, remember to slow down. Read each sentence carefully and make sure you understand the sentence before you read the next one.

Page 35

An energy company came to Marfork in the 1990s. It began a process called mountaintop removal mining. Using dynamite, the company blew off the tops of mountains to get at the large amounts of coal underneath. The process was quicker than the old method of digging for coal underground, but it caused many problems. Whole forests were destroyed.

I read that an energy company started a different process of getting coal. The company blows off the top of a mountain to get to the coal underneath.

Your Turn Why did Judy Bonds leave Marfork? Read page 36 of "Judy's Appalachia" to answer the question. As you read, remember to use the strategy Reread.

_____

_____

Timeline

The selection "Judy's Appalachia" is a biography.

A biography

- is the story of a real person's life written by another person
- usually presents events in sequence, or chronological order
- may include text features, such as timelines and photographs.

🔍 FIND TEXT EVIDENCE

You can tell "Judy's Appalachia" is a biography because the text describes a real person. The events in Judy's life are presented in chronological order. The story includes text features.

Page 36

Dust from the explosions filled the air and settled over the towns. Coal sludge, a mixture of mud, chemicals, and coal dust, got into the creeks and rivers.

Pollution from the mountaintop removal mining began making people living in the towns below the mountains sick. In the area where Judy lived, coal sludge flowed into the rivers and streams. People packed up and left. Judy was heartbroken. The land she loved was being **mistreated**. She realized that the valley that had always been her home had been poisoned. No longer a safe place to live, it had become dangerous. Judy, her daughter, and her grandson had to leave.

Working for Change

Something had to be done about the pollution. Judy decided it was important to **protest** against strip mining and demand that it be stopped. She felt that she must try to keep the area safe for people. She felt **qualified** to talk to groups about the **injustice** of whole towns being forced to move and mountains and forests being destroyed, all because of strip mining. After all, she had grown up in a mining family.

1952	2001	2003	2011
Judy is born in West Virginia.	Judy's family is forced to leave Marfork Hollow.	Judy is awarded the $150,000 Goldman Environmental Prize.	Judy dies at age 59.

Timeline

A timeline is a kind of diagram that shows events in the order in which they took place.

Your Turn Find and list two text features in "Judy's Appalachia." Tell your partner what information you learned from each of the features.

_____

_____

_____

Author's Point of View

Authors have a position, or point of view, about the topics they write about. Look for details in the text, such as the reasons and evidence the author chooses to present. This will help you to figure out the author's point of view.

FIND TEXT EVIDENCE

When I reread the first paragraph on page 35, I can look for details that reveal the author's point of view about Judy Bonds.

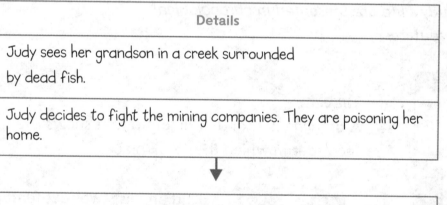

Details
Judy sees her grandson in a creek surrounded by dead fish.
Judy decides to fight the mining companies. They are poisoning her home.

↓

Author's Point of View
The author admires Judy Bonds for taking a stand against the coal mining companies.

Your Turn Reread "Judy's Appalachia." Look for two more details that help support the author's point of view and list them in your graphic organizer on page 43.

SeanPavonePhoto/Getty Images

Details

↓

Author's Purpose

Respond to Reading

COLLABORATE

Discuss the prompt below. Think about how the author describes Judy's life. Use your notes and graphic organizer.

How would "Judy's Appalachia" be different if the author had a different point of view? What if the author did not believe that coal mining was a threat to the environment? _____

_____

_____

_____

_____

_____

_____

_____

_____

_____

_____

_____

_____

Paraphrasing

When you research a topic, you find information from many different sources. As you take notes, it is important to **paraphrase**, or restate the information in your own words. Copying other people's ideas and words without giving them credit is called "plagiarism."

To paraphrase what you read:

- Think about the meaning of the paragraph.
- Restate the information in your own words.

Paraphrase this description of Texas Congresswoman Barbara Jordan: *Jordan was an extraordinary orator who was known for her powerful speeches.*

_____

_____

COLLABORATE

Make a Book Cover With a partner, research a historical figure who has played an important role in your state's government. Ask your teacher or a librarian to help you plan your research. Use your research to make a book cover for a biography of that person.

- As you research, take notes and paraphrase the information you learn about your historical figure from each source.

- On the front cover, add an illustration or photo of that person. On the inside flap, describe this person's achievements. On the back cover, write a persuasive summary of why this person made a difference in your state. You may wish to create your book cover online. After you finish, share your work with the class.

Library of Congress Prints and Photographs Division (LC-U9-32937-32A/33)

Delivering Justice

? **How does the author help you visualize how Westley and Grandma were treated at Levy's?**

Literature Anthology: pages 196–213

Talk About It Reread page 199 of the **Literature Anthology**. Talk to your partner about what happened to Westley and Grandma at Levy's.

Cite Text Evidence What words does the author use to help you picture what happened? Write text evidence here.

Make Inferences

Think about how the saleswoman treats Westley's Grandma on page 199. Then think about Grandma's words and actions. What inferences can you make about Grandma?

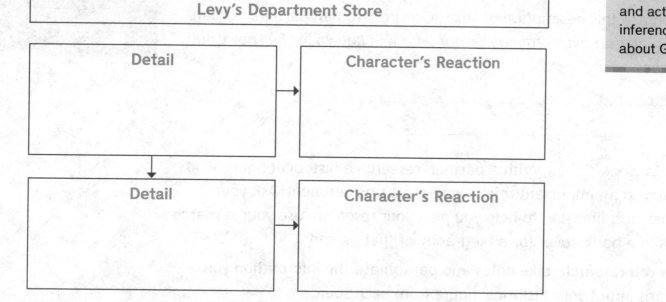

Levy's Department Store

Detail		Character's Reaction
	→	

Detail		Character's Reaction

Write The author helps me see how Westley and Grandma were treated at Levy's by _____

_____

_____

? **How do you know what kind of person Westley is?**

Talk About It Reread page 203 of the **Literature Anthology**. Turn to your partner and talk about Westley's role in voter registration.

Cite Text Evidence What do Westley's actions show about his character? What inferences can you make about Westley? Cite text evidence in the chart.

How Westley Helps	What This Shows

Write The author helps me understand what kind of person Westley is by

_____

_____

_____

? **How does the illustration help you understand what a boycott is?**

Talk About It Look at the illustration on **Literature Anthology** page 208. Reread page 209. Discuss what the people are doing.

Cite Text Evidence What clues in the illustration and the text help you understand what a boycott is? Write evidence in the chart.

Illustration Clues	Text Clues	How They Help

Write The author uses the illustration to help me understand that a boycott is _____

_____

_____

Quick Tip

Use these sentence starters to help you talk about the illustration on page 208.

• *The people in the picture are . . .*

• *The people are carrying . . .*

• *There is a pile of . . .*

Synthesize Information

Combine the information from the text you have read so far and the illustration to develop your understanding. Why are people boycotting the shops on Broughton Street? Look at all the charge cards in the illustration. Why might this boycott be an effective way to create change?

Respond to Reading

COLLABORATE

Discuss the prompt below. Think about how each event affected Westley. Use your notes and graphic organizer.

How does the author, Jim Haskins, use the events in Westley's life to show how they helped Westley to become a leader in his community?

_____

_____

_____

_____

_____

_____

_____

_____

_____

_____

_____

_____

Keeping Freedom in the Family

Literature Anthology:
pages 216–219

1   As I held on to my father's hand, we joined the line of people chanting and walking back and forth in a picket line in front of Lawrence Hospital. The year was 1965, and the hospital workers needed more money and better working conditions. So there we were on a cold Saturday afternoon to protest. When I looked up, I saw soldiers on the roof of the hospital. I squeezed Daddy's hand a little tighter. The soldiers were there to protect us, he said. We were American citizens, and we had the right to gather and to protest. I raised my picket sign as high as I could. I wasn't afraid. I had Daddy and the American Constitution to protect me.

Circle words that describe the picket line.

Underline why Nora and her family are participating in the protest. Write the reason here:

_____

_____

_____

_____

COLLABORATE

Talk with a partner about how Nora feels. **Draw a box** around text evidence that supports your ideas.

1   When four black girls were killed in a church bombing in Alabama, we realized that the fight for change would be hard, long, and dangerous. Mom and Dad encouraged us to think about how we could protest the bombing. Some people said we should boycott Christmas. This was our first Christmas in the new house, and the spirit of giving was important to us.

2   So instead of boycotting Christmas, our family decided to boycott Christmas shopping. Instead of buying gifts, our family gave the money to civil rights groups. Guy, La Verne, and I gave each other gifts we had made with our own hands. And when the time came to hang the home-made paper holiday chain, I wrote the names of the girls in the last four loops. In our own small way, we learned the true meaning of giving.

3   When we gathered for dinner that night, we said a special prayer for the girls and for our country—and I knew that Christmas at the Davis house would never be the same.

Reread paragraph 1. **Underline** how the author helps you understand that protesting the bombing was important to her family. Then reread paragraph 2. **Circle** how Nora and her family chose to protest.

COLLABORATE

Reread paragraph 3. Talk with a partner about why "Christmas at the Davis house would never be the same." **Put checkmarks** in the margin beside the text evidence that supports this.

How does the author help you visualize what it was like to walk in a picket line?

COLLABORATE

Talk About It Reread the excerpt on page 50. Talk with a partner about what happened at the protest.

Cite Text Evidence What words help you picture how walking in the picket line felt to Nora? Write text evidence in the web.

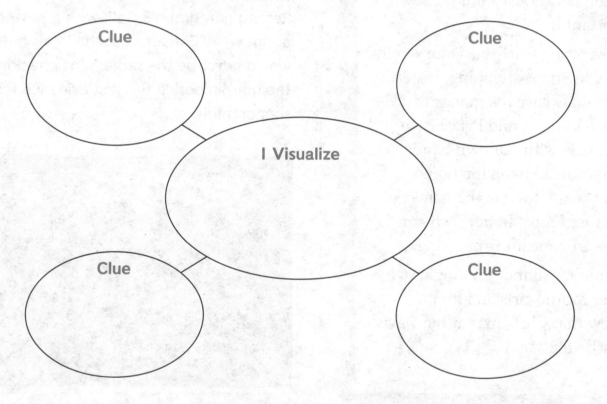

Clue

Clue

I Visualize

Clue

Clue

Write I can visualize what the picket line was like because the author

_____

_____

_____

Anecdote

Sometimes writers will use a brief story, or **anecdote**, to begin a speech or personal narrative. An anecdote can entertain, inform, persuade, or inspire. To grab the reader's attention, authors often write the anecdote in the first-person point of view, and they use sensory details.

🔍 FIND TEXT EVIDENCE

Read the introduction below from "Keeping Freedom in the Family." Notice how Nora Davis Day writes in the first person. The first-person voice helps the reader experience the events up close.

> As I held on to my father's hand, we joined the line of people chanting and walking back and forth in a picket line in front of Lawrence Hospital.

Your Turn Reread the paragraph of "Keeping Freedom in the Family" on page 50. Think about the scene that the author describes.

- What can you infer or tell about the author from the above paragraph? _____

    _____

- What is the author's purpose for using this anecdote to begin her autobiography?_____

    _____

Wuttichok Panichiwarapun/Shutterstock.com

Text Connections

? **Think about the selections you have read. How did the people in those selections make a difference?**

COLLABORATE

Talk About It With a partner, read the poem. Talk about what Paul Revere plans to do if the British invade.

Cite Text Evidence **Circle** words and phrases that describe the actions of Paul Revere's plan. **Underline** the words that show what the people will do if Paul Revere spreads the alarm.

Write The selections that I read and the poem help me understand that people can make a difference by _____

_____

_____

_____

_____

_____

_____

_____

_____

_____

Quick Tip

Use these sentence starters to talk about the selections you have read.

- *Westley made a difference by . . .*
- *Nora Davis Day learned . . .*
- *Paul Revere made a difference by . . .*

from *Paul Revere's Ride*

He said to his friend, "If the British march
By land or sea from the town to-night,
Hang a lantern aloft in the belfry-arch
Of the North-Church-tower, as a signal-light,—
One if by land, and two if by sea;
And I on the opposite shore will be,
Ready to ride and spread the alarm
Through every Middlesex village and farm,
For the country-folk to be up and to arm."

— Henry Wadsworth Longfellow

Present Your Work

COLLABORATE

Discuss how you will present your book cover to your class. Practice your presentation with a partner. Discuss the sentence starters below and write your answers. Use the Listening Checklist when your classmates give their presentation.

The state historical figure we chose was important because_____

_____

_____

I will pay more attention to the information on book covers from now on because _____

_____

_____

✓ Listening Checklist

- ☐ During the presentation, listen to the speaker carefully.
- ☐ Take notes on one or two things you liked.
- ☐ Pay attention to how the speaker uses the visuals.
- ☐ After the presentation, tell why you liked the presentation.
- ☐ If someone else makes the same comment first, tell why you agree.

Talk About It

Essential Question

In what ways can advances in science be helpful or harmful?

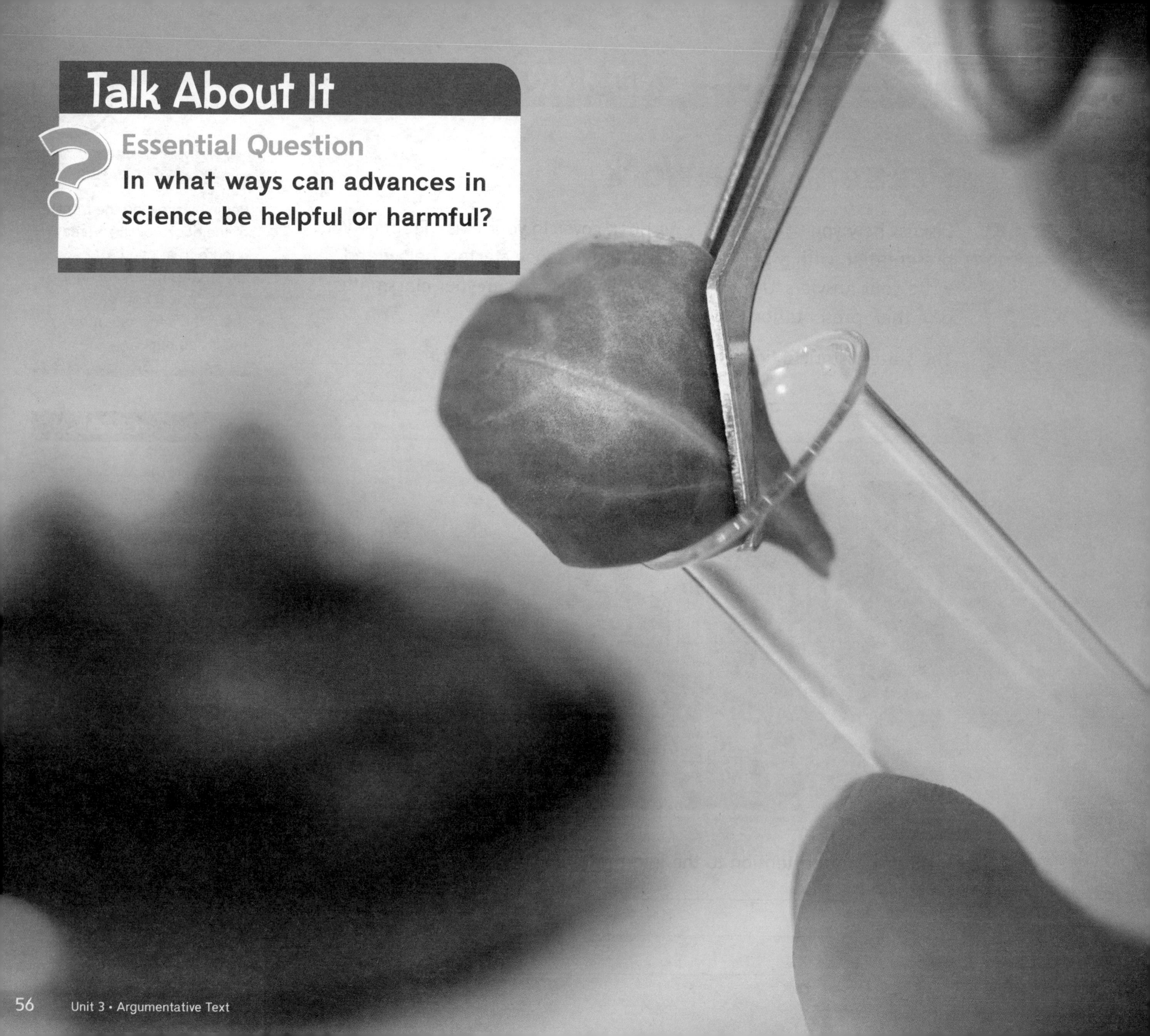

COLLABORATE

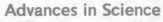
SCIENCE

Scientific discoveries have led to disease-resistant crops. Some people believe these discoveries will help solve world hunger. Others believe these new foods will cause more harm than good.

Discuss the things you think scientists should research. How would the research be helpful? Then discuss the problems it may cause. As you express your opinion, enunciate, or speak clearly. Then write your ideas in the web.

Advances in Science

BLAST BACK!
studysync

Go online to **my.mheducation.com** and read the "Fertilizers: The Good and the Bad" blast. Why is knowing two points of view important? What is your opinion about fertilizers? Blast back your response.

TAKE NOTES

Asking questions helps you figure out your purpose for reading. It also gives you a chance to think about what you know about the topic. Before you read, write a question here.

_____

_____

_____

As you read, make note of:

Interesting Words _____

_____

_____

_____

Key Details _____

_____

_____

_____

_____

_____

_____

Essential Question

In what ways can advances in science be helpful or harmful?

Read about how science has helped to change food crops.

Food Fight

Annabelle Breckey/Digital Vision/Getty Images

Is it safe to interfere with Mother Nature?

Some scientists use a technique called genetic modification to make "superior" food crops. It involves altering a seed's genes. Genes are the "instruction codes" that all living things have inside their cells. A seed's genetic code sets what **characteristics** it will **inherit** when it grows into a plant, such as how big it will grow and the nutrients it will contain.

For thousands of years, farmers made crops better by crossbreeding plants. They would add pollen from the sweetest melon plants to the flowers of plants that produced the biggest melons. This process would make new plants with big, sweet melons. But this crossbreeding process does not always work, and its cycle can take years to get good results.

But advances in gene science have created shortcuts. Using new tools, scientists can put a gene from one living thing into another.

That living thing could be a plant, a bacterium, a virus, or even an animal. These foods are called genetically modified foods, or GM foods. The goal of GM foods is to create foods that can survive insects or harsh conditions or can grow faster. But are these **advancements** in **agriculture** good for us?

ARGUMENTATIVE TEXT

FIND TEXT EVIDENCE

Read

Paragraphs 1–2

Greek Roots

The Greek root *techn-* means "method" or "system." **Circle** a word with the Greek root *techn-* in it. What other words do you know that include this word part?

Author's Point of View

Underline the sentence that shows the author's point of view about crossbreeding.

Paragraphs 3–4

Reread

Draw a box around the text that tells what kinds of living things scientists take genes from.

Reread

Author's Craft

What is the author's purpose for questioning if the advancements in agriculture will be good for us?

FIND TEXT EVIDENCE 🔍

Read

Paragraphs 1–3

Author's Point of View

Underline the sentence that tells you what the author thinks about Bt corn.

Reread

Draw a box around text that tells why the author thinks genetically modified rice is a good thing.

Sidebar

Headings

Write the headings shown in the sidebar on the lines below. **Circle** how each food was improved.

_____

_____

Reread

Author's Craft

What facts does the author use to support his argument for GM foods?

Support for Superfoods

Scientists believe the new techniques can create crops with a **resistance** to pests and disease. Bt corn is a genetically modified corn.

It has an insect-killing gene that comes from a bacterium. Farmers who grow Bt corn can use fewer chemicals while they grow their crops. That is good for the environment.

Disease-resistant GM potatoes were introduced in the 1990s.

Some superfoods are extra nutritious. Golden rice has been genetically modified with three different genes. One gene is a form of bacterium. The other two are from daffodils. The new genes help the rice to make a nutrient that prevents some forms of blindness.

Superfoods

These foods may seem common. But did you know that the genetically modified versions have special powers?

Rice

Rice contains phytic acid. Too much of this acid can be bad for people. A new type of rice has been bred with a low level of phytic acid.

Salmon

To create supersized salmon, scientists changed the gene that controls growth. The genetically altered salmon grow twice as fast as their wild cousins.

Tomatoes

Genetically engineered tomatoes can be picked when they are ripe and still not bruise when shipped. One food company tried to use an arctic flounder fish gene to create a tomato that could survive frost. The fish-tomato did not succeed.

MAP KEY

Percentage of people that are not getting enough food

- ☐ Over 35%
- ☐ 20-34%
- ☐ 10-19%
- ☐ 5-9%
- ☐ Less than 5%
- ☐ Not enough data

Safety Issues

Many people have **disagreed** that GM foods are a good idea. They worry that GM foods will hurt the environment and humans. One concern is that plants with new genes will crossbreed with weeds to make pesticide-resistant weeds. Another concern is that GM foods may trigger allergies.

Genetically modified crops are **prevalent** in the U.S. But some people will not buy them because of health **concerns**. GM foods can leave foreign material inside us, causing lifelong problems.

As a result, many companies avoid GM foods.

The Long Term

Genetically modified foods pollute the environment forever because it is impossible to fully clean up a contaminated gene pool. It is important to keep researching GM foods because these types of foods can create dangerous side effects.

Summarize

Use your notes and the map to help you summarize "Food Fight."

FIND TEXT EVIDENCE

Read

Map

Look at the map. **Underline** the countries where less than 5% of the people are not getting enough food. In what parts of Africa are these countries located?

_____

_____

Paragraphs 1–3

Author's Point of View

Circle the sentences that tell you what the author's claim is about the health concerns with GM foods. Write the claim below.

_____

_____

_____

Reread

Author's Craft

What is the author's purpose for including the section "The Long Term"?

Vocabulary

Use the example sentences to talk with a partner about each word. Then answer the questions.

advancements

The latest **advancements** in technology have improved cell phones.

What advancements in technology have you heard about recently?

_____

_____

agriculture

Jaime studied **agriculture** to learn how to grow more crops on his farm.

Why is agriculture important?

_____

_____

characteristics

Feathers and wings are two characteristics of a bird.

What characteristics does a cat have?

_____

_____

concerns

I had **concerns** about my dog's health.

What have you had concerns about?

_____

_____

disagreed

The brothers **disagreed** about whose turn it was to wash the dishes.

What have you disagreed with someone about?

_____

_____

Build Your Word List Pick one of the interesting words you noted on page 58 and look up its meaning in a print or digital dictionary. Then in your writer's notebook make a word web with synonyms, antonyms, and related words.

inherit

Mom hopes the baby will **inherit** her red hair.

What other characteristics can we inherit from our parents?

_____

_____

prevalent

Snowstorms are **prevalent** in the northeast in the winter.

What kind of weather is prevalent where you live in springtime?

_____

_____

resistance

Brushing and flossing your teeth can build up a **resistance** to tooth decay.

How can you build up a resistance to an illness?

_____

Greek Roots

Knowing Greek roots can help you figure out the meanings of unfamiliar words. Here are some common Greek roots that may help you as you read "Food Fight."

gen = race, kind   *techn* = art, skill, method
agr = field   *chron* = time

🔍 FIND TEXT EVIDENCE

When I read the word cycle *on page 59, I know the Greek root* cycl *means "circle." Cycle* must mean "a series of events that repeat regularly."

But this crossbreeding process does not always work, and its cycle can take years to get good results.

Your Turn Use Greek roots and context clues to find the meanings of the following words from "Food Fight."

gene, *page 59* _____

_____

agriculture, *page 59* _____

_____

Reread

"Food Fight" is an argumentative text. In an argumentative text, a writer has an opinion about a topic. The writer makes a claim and provides facts to support the claim. The writer wants to convince the reader to agree with his or her opinion. Reread the text to make sure you understand the claims and supporting facts.

Quick Tip

If you read something you don't understand, write down or underline the text. Read the text again slowly, stopping after each sentence to make sure you understand it. Look up any words that you do not understand.

FIND TEXT EVIDENCE

You may not be sure about identifying a claim and a supporting fact. Reread the last paragraph on page 60 of "Food Fight," which makes a claim and gives a supporting fact.

Page 60

> Some superfoods are extra nutritious. Golden rice has been genetically modified with three different genes. One gene is a form of bacterium. The other two are from daffodils. The new genes help the rice to make a nutrient that prevents some forms of blindness.

I read the claim that golden rice is extra nutritious. The fact that supports the claim is that golden rice has been genetically modified with three different genes. The new genes help the rice make a nutrient that prevents some forms of blindness.

Your Turn Explain how the author supports his opinion that GM foods are not a good idea. Reread "Safety Issues" on page 61 to answer the question. As you read, remember to use the strategy Reread.

_____

_____

Maps and Headings

An argumentative text is nonfiction and may give two different points of view about a topic. Argumentative text may include text features, such as maps and headings. For example, the headings "Support for Superfoods" and "Safety Issues" give different points of view. These features help to persuade the reader to agree with the author's opinion.

FIND TEXT EVIDENCE

"Food Fight" is an argumentative text that gives reasons for and against GM foods. It includes text features, such as headings and maps, to help support the author's opinion and claims.

Page 61

MAP KEY
Percentage of people that are not getting enough food

☐ Over 35%
☐ 20-34%
☐ 10-19%
☐ 5-9%
☐ Less than 5%
☐ Not enough data

Safety Issues

Many people have **disagreed** that GM foods are a good idea. They worry that GM foods will hurt the environment and humans. One concern is that plants with new genes will crossbreed with weeds to make pesticide-resistant weeds. Another concern is that GM foods may trigger allergies.

Genetically modified crops are **prevalent** in the U.S. But some people will not buy them because of health **concerns**. GM foods can leave foreign material inside us, causing lifelong problems.

As a result, many companies avoid GM foods.

The Long Term

Genetically modified foods pollute the environment forever because it is impossible to fully clean up a contaminated gene pool. It is important to keep researching GM foods because these types of foods can create dangerous side effects.

Summarize

 Use your notes and the map to help you summarize "Food Fight."

Maps

Maps show geographic locations of specific areas of the world. They usually include a map key and a compass rose.

Headings

Headings tell you what the section is mostly about.

Your Turn Find two other text features in "Food Fight." Tell what information you learned from each feature.

_____

_____

_____

Author's Point of View

Authors have a point of view, or opinion, on the topics they write about. Look for details in the text, such as the reasons and claims the author chooses to present. This will help you to figure out the author's point of view.

🔍 FIND TEXT EVIDENCE

When I reread page 60 of "Food Fight," I can identify details in the text that explain and support the author's claim or opinion. Then I can figure out the author's point of view.

Details
Farmers who grow BT corn use fewer chemicals.
Using fewer chemicals is good for the environment.
Some GM foods have been created to be extra nutritious.

↓

Author's Point of View

Your Turn Reread page 61. Find the important details in the section and list them in your graphic organizer on page 67. Use the details to determine the author's point of view.

Maks Narodenko/Shutterstock.com

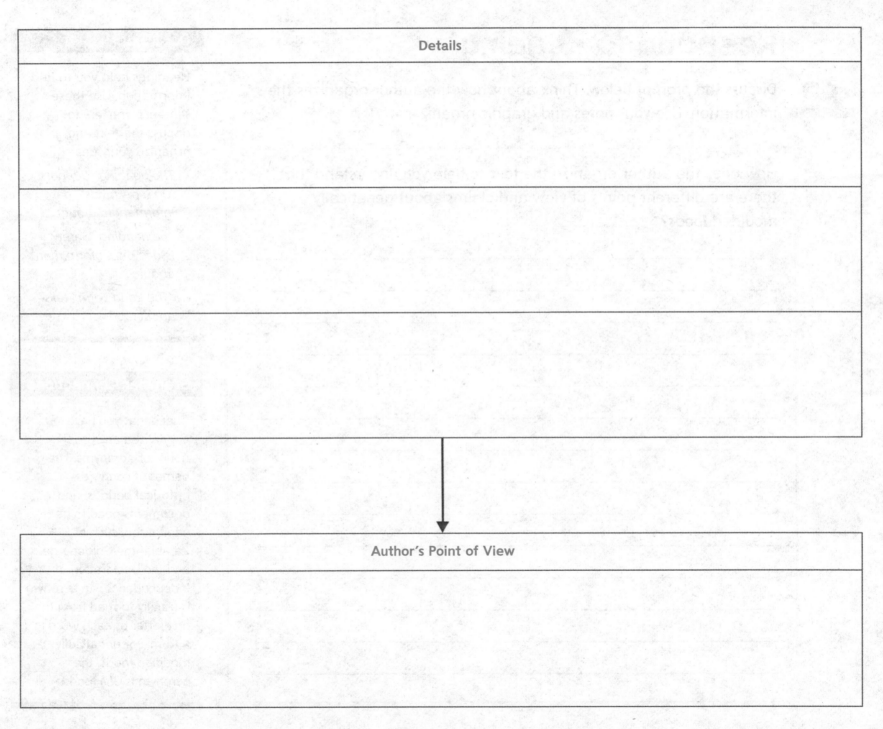

Details

Author's Point of View

Respond to Reading

Discuss the prompt below. Think about how the author organizes the information. Use your notes and graphic organizer.

How does the author organize the text to help you understand that there are different points of view and claims about genetically modified foods?

_____

_____

_____

_____

_____

_____

_____

_____

_____

_____

_____

_____

SCIENCE

How to Read a Diagram

Diagrams are drawings that show the appearance or parts of something, or how something works. Diagrams usually include labels that identify each part. A writer may use a diagram to show you visually what the text says or to give more information. To read a diagram

- look closely at each part
- follow the arrows to see the sequence of each stage
- read each label and any caption
- note any additional information not in the written text

The diagram on this page is about the life cycle of tomatoes. What could you make a diagram about? Write it here.

_____

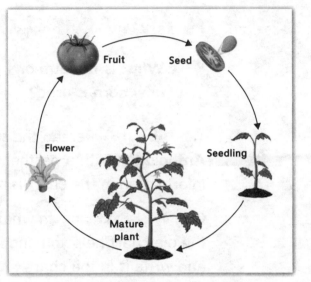

The diagram above shows the life cycle of a tomato plant. What happens to a seed? Write your answer below.

_____

COLLABORATE

Make a Slide Show With a partner or in a group, research a main agricultural crop in your state. Use a variety of sources. Then create a slide show about the crop. Include a diagram and these facts:

- the crop's life cycle
- how much of the crop is raised each year
- where and how the crop is shipped

Make sure your diagram has labels and your pictures have captions to help readers understand the process. Finally, share your work with the class.

A New Kind of Corn

Literature Anthology:
pages 220–223

? **What is the author's purpose for including a pie chart to show how corn is used?**

COLLABORATE

Talk About It Reread the sidebar on page 221 of the **Literature Anthology**. With a partner, analyze the pie chart. Talk about how the information in the chart is related to all of the text on the page.

Cite Text Evidence In what ways does the information in the text and the pie chart help you understand more about Bt corn? Find evidence and write it in the chart.

Evaluating Information

In an argumentative text, the author must provide evidence to support his or her claim. How would you check the information in the pie chart to see if it is reliable?

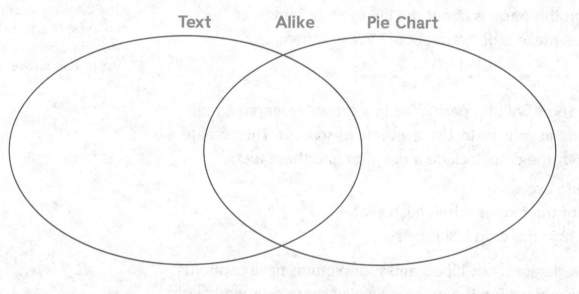

Text   Alike   Pie Chart

Write The author uses the sidebar with the pie chart to _____

_____

_____

? **How do the authors of both argumentative text articles help you understand what they think?**

Talk About It Reread the two articles on pages 222 and 223 of the **Literature Anthology**. Turn to a partner and talk about the different perspectives and claims presented in the articles.

Cite Text Evidence What evidence helps you understand the points of view of the farmer and the consumer? Write text evidence in the chart.

Quick Tip

You can use these sentence starters when you talk about the two different perspectives.

- *The farmer explains that planting Bt corn has . . .*
- *The consumer explains that Bt corn . . .*

Bt Corn Is Better	Bt Corn Could Be Bad
Point of View	Point of View

Write The intended audience for the argumentative articles is_____

_____

Respond to Reading

COLLABORATE

Discuss the prompt below. Apply your own knowledge of how science can be helpful or harmful. Use your notes and graphic organizer.

How does the way the author presents two different points of view help you understand more about GM foods?

_____

_____

_____

_____

_____

_____

_____

_____

_____

_____

_____

_____

_____

_____

Self-Selected Reading

Choose a text. Read the first two pages. If five or more words are unfamiliar, pick another text. Fill in your writer's notebook with the title, author, genre, and your purpose for reading.

The Pick of the Patch

Literature Anthology:
pages 224–225

1   This world record-breaking pumpkin tipped the scales at more than 1,810 pounds. What is the secret to growing a giant gourd? According to record-breaker Chris Stevens, "Sunshine, rain, cow manure, fish [fertilizer], and seaweed." Read on for a recipe you can recreate at home.

2   Growing a giant pumpkin takes knowledge and skill. Follow these six simple steps to grow your own great gourd.

1. Study up on seeds.

Some popular pumpkin seeds that get big results include Prizewinner Hybrid, Atlantic Giant, Mammoth Gold, and Big Max. Many are sold online for just $1.

2. Take your time.

Giant pumpkins need time to grow. May is a good month to plant seeds in a pot. Let them make advancements in that safe space before you transplant them outside. Plant them in good quality soil and fertilize them well.

Reread paragraph 1. **Underline** how the author gets you interested in reading more about how to grow a giant pumpkin.

Reread paragraph 2. **Circle** what it takes to grow a giant pumpkin. Write the answers here:

_____

_____

_____

_____

Talk with a partner about how the author helps you understand how to grow a giant pumpkin. **Draw a box** around how he helps you understand what each step is going to be about.

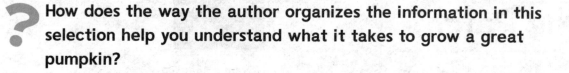

? How does the way the author organizes the information in this selection help you understand what it takes to grow a great pumpkin?

COLLABORATE

Talk About It Reread the excerpt on page 73. Talk with a partner about what you learned from the author about how to get started growing a big pumpkin.

Cite Text Evidence What does the author write about that makes you want to know how to grow a 1,810-pound pumpkin? Write text evidence in the chart.

What the Author Does	How it Helps

Write The author helps me understand how to grow a great pumpkin by

_____

_____

_____

_____

Procedural Text

All **procedural text** has step-by-step directions that explain how to do something. A recipe is an example of a procedural text. Often the steps are numbered or the text has words such as *first, next, then,* and *finally.* Sometimes the author includes more detailed information, such as what kinds of seeds to use.

FIND TEXT EVIDENCE

On page 225 of "The Pick of the Patch" in the **Literature Anthology,** the author gives a brief introduction that explains how many steps it will take to grow a large pumpkin.

> Growing a giant pumpkin takes knowledge and skill. Follow these six simple steps to grow your own great gourd.

Your Turn Reread Steps 5 and 6 on page 225.

- How can you give a pumpkin a better chance to grow? Write it here.

  _____

  _____

- How long should you water and fertilize pumpkins? Write it here.

  _____

  _____

When you write procedural text, choose precise words that clearly explain what to do. Write a list of steps to make it easy for readers to follow. You can begin each step with an imperative (command) verb, such as *take, put, cut,* or *open.* Think of a word that will answer the reader's question: "What do I do next?"

Text Connections

? How does the author organize the lyrics in the song? How did the authors of "A New Kind of Corn" and "The Pick of the Patch" organize their articles?

Talk About It Read the lyrics of the song. Talk about how the writer shows that there are two voices, and therefore two points of view.

Cite Text Evidence **Circle** the lyrics that show one point of view. Then **underline** the phrases that show the other point of view. Think about how the authors of the selections you read this week use organization to share information and points of view.

Write The songwriter organizes the information like

_____

_____

_____

_____

_____

_____

Quick Tip

Note how the songwriter organizes the lyrics into two voices. This will help you compare the song to other texts.

"Did You Feed My Cow?"

(lyrics)

Did you feed my cow?
(Yes, Ma-am)

Could you tell me how?
(Yes, Ma-am)

What did you feed her?
(Corn and hay)

What did you feed her?
(Corn and hay)

Did you milk her good?
(Yes, Ma-am)

Now did you milk her like you should?
(Yes, Ma-am)

How did you milk her?
(Squish, squish, squish)

How did you milk her?
(Squish, squish, squish)

Accuracy and Rate

When you read expository or argumentative text aloud, accuracy (or being precise) is important. Look up the pronunciation of any unfamiliar words and practice them until you can read the text with accuracy. Try not to read too quickly or slowly. If you read too quickly, the listener may hear only the words and not the meaning of the sentences. Read at a rate, or speed, that helps the listener understand what you are saying.

Quick Tip

If you are having trouble pronouncing a word, look it up in a print or digital dictionary. Pronounce each syllable in the word clearly. Some digital dictionaries may have audio for you to hear how a word is pronounced.

Page 60

Some superfoods are extra nutritious. Golden rice has been genetically modified with three different genes. One gene is a form of bacterium. The other two are from daffodils. The new genes help the rice to make a nutrient that prevents some forms of blindness.

Look up the pronunciation of unfamiliar words and practice saying them.

Your Turn Take turns reading page 60 of "Food Fight" aloud with a partner. Record each other, then listen to the playback. Write down any problems with accuracy and rate. Then record yourselves again.

Afterward, think about how you did. Complete these sentences.

I remembered to _____

_____

Next time I will _____

_____

Literature Anthology:
Pages 220-223

Expert Model

Features of an Opinion Essay

An opinion essay is a form of argumentative text. Authors of argumentative text share their opinions or claims with readers and try to persuade them to agree with that opinion. Opinion writing

- has an introduction that clearly states the author's opinion about a topic

- contains reasons, facts, and examples that support that opinion

- includes a strong conclusion to convince readers to agree with that opinion

Analyze an Expert Model Studying argumentative texts will help you learn how to write an opinion essay. **Reread** page 221 of *A New Kind of Corn* in the **Literature Anthology**. Write your answers to the questions below.

What is the writer's opinion about this topic? _____

_____

_____

Identify the audience for this article and explain your answer.

_____

_____

_____

Word Wise

On page 221, the author uses the words *unnecessary* and *appealing*. These words signal an opinion. Some people might not agree that the sweetener is unnecessary or that Bt corn is appealing. Examples of other words that signal an opinion are: *believe, feel, think, worst, best,* and *the most.*

Plan: Choose Your Topic

Brainstorm With a partner or a small group, brainstorm a list of electronic things you use that have screens. Discuss how much time you spend looking at these screens each week. Write the time next to each device.

_____

_____

_____

Writing Prompt Look over your list. Write an opinion essay about how much time you think students should be allowed to spend on screens.

My opinion is that students should_____

_____

Purpose and Audience An **author's purpose** is his or her main reason for writing. Look at the three purposes for writing below. Underline your purpose for writing an opinion essay.

   to inform, or teach   to persuade, or convince   to entertain

Think about the audience for your essay. Who will read it?

My audience will be _____.

I will give _____ to support my opinion essay.

Plan In your writer's notebook, write what your opinion is about screen time. Use a graphic organizer to write down details that support your opinion.

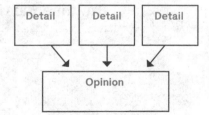

Detail	Detail	Detail

Opinion

Plan: Strong Introductions

State Your Opinion A strong introduction to an opinion essay introduces the topic and clearly states the writer's opinion. In order to grab the reader's attention, a strong introduction may also include

- a fascinating fact

- a thoughtful question

- an amusing story or anecdote

Write a fact, question, or anecdote that will get your reader's attention.

_____

_____

_____

Take Notes Do research in the library or online to get facts or quotes from experts to support your opinion. Then make a list of the ones that you might want to use for your opening statement. Organize your notes by writing them in your graphic organizer.

Digital Tools

For more information on writing an opinion, watch the "Opinion Statement" tutorial. Go to **my.mheducation.com**.

Draft

Relevant Evidence Writers support their opinions with evidence such as facts, reasons, and examples. All the evidence must be **relevant**, or relate to the topic. In the example below from "Food Fight," the author uses only details that relate to the topic.

> Scientists believe the new techniques can create crops with a resistance to pests and disease. Bt corn is a genetically modified corn.
>
> It has an insect-killing gene that comes from a bacterium. Farmers who grow Bt corn can use fewer chemicals while they grow their crops. That is good for the environment.

Use the above passage as a model to write a paragraph of your opinion essay. As you write, ask yourself: Is this evidence relevant? How does the evidence support my opinion?

_____

_____

_____

_____

_____

_____

 Write a Draft Use your graphic organizer to help you write your draft in your writer's notebook. Remember to start with a strong introduction and provide evidence to support your opinion. Be sure to check your draft for any unnecessary details and ideas.

Quick Tip

Writers add, delete, combine, and rearrange sentences in their drafts. They delete any unnecessary details and ideas. How do you know if evidence is relevant? It has to stay on topic. Read these sentences:

Bill has too much screen time. He watches lots of TV shows. He gets lots of text messages on his cell phone. Bill likes to swim. He reads ebooks on his tablet.

Which sentence is not relevant?

Revise

Strong Conclusions A strong conclusion restates the reasons and evidence that support the writer's claim or opinion. Read the paragraph below. Then revise the last sentence to make the conclusion strong enough to convince readers to agree with the writer's opinion.

> I believe we need laws to control the use of camera phones. People take pictures on camera phones without our consent. Sometimes the pictures show people at bad moments like when they are slipping or falling. Then the pictures get uploaded to the Internet, where it can be embarrassing for the people in the picture. That is not right.

_____

_____

_____

_____

Revision As you revise your draft, make sure you have a strong opening and a strong conclusion. Confirm that you have enough relevant facts and examples to support your opinion.

Grammar Connections

Varying sentences can strengthen your essay. Ask a question at the beginning of a paragraph: *How much time do you spend on screens?* Try adding an exclamation: *Forty hours a week!* Or try beginning a sentence with a verb: *Watching television . . .*

If your sentences are all the same length, combine sentences to make compound sentences. Or make a longer sentence shorter. Writing different kinds of sentences will keep your reader interested!

Peer Conferences

COLLABORATE

Review a Draft Listen carefully as a partner reads his or her work aloud. Take notes about what you liked and what was difficult to follow. Begin by telling what you liked about the draft. Ask questions that will help the writer think more about the writing. Make suggestions you think will make the writing stronger. Use these sentence starters.

I enjoyed your strong introduction because . . .

Another relevant fact you might add is . . .

This part is unclear to me. Can you explain . . . ?

Partner Feedback After your partner gives you feedback on your draft, write one of the suggestions that you will use in your revision. Refer to the rubric on page 85 as you give feedback.

Based on my partner's feedback, I will _____

_____

_____

After you finish giving each other feedback, reflect on the peer conference. What was helpful? What might you do differently next time?

Revision As you revise your draft, use the Revising Checklist to help you figure out what text you may need to move, elaborate on, or delete. Remember to use the rubric on page 85 to help with your revision.

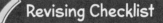

Revising Checklist

- [ ] Did I begin with a clear and strong introduction about my opinion?
- [ ] Did I give enough relevant evidence for my opinion?
- [ ] Did I present information in an organized way?
- [ ] Did I end with a strong conclusion?

Edit and Proofread

When you **edit** and **proofread** your writing, you look for and correct mistakes in spelling, punctuation, capitalization, and grammar. Reading through a revised draft multiple times can help you make sure you're catching any errors. Use the checklist below to edit your sentences.

✔ Editing Checklist

- ☐ Do all sentences begin with a capital letter and end with a punctuation mark?
- ☐ Are proper nouns capitalized?
- ☐ Is there noun and verb agreement?
- ☐ Are possessive nouns and contractions used correctly?
- ☐ Are quotation marks used correctly?
- ☐ Are irregular verbs spelled correctly?

List two mistakes you found as you proofread your essay.

1 _____

_____

2 _____

_____

Tech Tip

Grammar checkers are useful tools in word-processing programs, but they may not always catch your punctuation mistakes.

Do a punctuation check of your opinion essay. Make sure each statement ends with a period. Questions need to end with a question mark. And statements of surprise or excitement should end with an exclamation mark.

Also, make sure you use commas correctly and put quotations marks before and after any actual quotes from experts.

Publish, Present, and Evaluate

Publishing When you **publish** your writing, you create a clean, neat final copy that is free of mistakes. Consider including an illustration of the topic to make your opinion essay more interesting. You might choose to draw a cartoon that conveys your opinion.

Presentation When you are ready to **present** your work, rehearse reading your essay aloud for a friend. Remember to use the appropriate volume. Use the Presenting Checklist to help you.

Evaluate After you publish your writing, use the rubric below to **evaluate** your writing.

What did you do successfully? _____

What needs more work? _____

_____

✓ Presenting Checklist

- ☐ Stand up straight.
- ☐ Look at your audience.
- ☐ Enunciate, or speak slowly and clearly.
- ☐ Speak loud enough, using appropriate volume, to communicate your ideas effectively.
- ☐ Pause to emphasize your relevant points.
- ☐ Read your conclusion with expression to convince the audience.

4	3	2	1
• gives a clear opinion with many pieces of relevant supporting evidence • makes it clear that the writer's purpose is to persuade readers • has a strong introduction and a strong conclusion	• gives a clear opinion with relevant supporting evidence • most of the writing shows a purpose to persuade readers • has a satisfactory introduction and conclusion	• gives an opinion with limited relevant supporting evidence • makes an effort to persuade readers • introduction and conclusion missing key details	• gives an opinion but lacks relevant supporting evidence • does not try to persuade readers • weak introduction and lacks precise conclusion

⟳ Spiral Review

You have learned new skills and strategies in Unit 3 that will help you read more critically. Now it is time to practice what you have learned.

- **Author's Point of View**
- **Author's Purpose**
- **Context Clues**
- **Flashback**
- **Point of View**
- **Sequence**
- **Antonyms**
- **Timeline**

Connect to Content

- **Draw a Map**
- **Watch a Primary Source**
- **Write Directions**

Read the selection and choose the best answer to each question.

A Political Pioneer: ANN RICHARDS

1   In 2003, Ann Richards said, "...to make things change for the better, that's a lifelong pursuit." Ann's lifelong pursuit was filled with passion and energy.

Early Life

2   Dorothy Ann Willis was born September 1, 1933, in Lakeview, Texas. She graduated from high school in 1950. Using a debating scholarship, she attended Baylor University. In the next few years, she got married, graduated, and received a teaching license. Richards said that teaching was the hardest work she did. For twenty years, Richards helped raise four children, while working in politics.

Ann Richards after being sworn in as the 45th Governor of Texas.

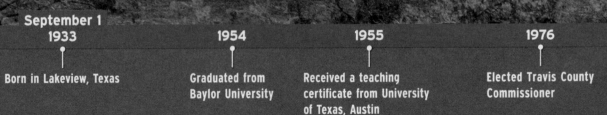

Ann Richards' Career

September 1 1933	1954	1955	1976
Born in Lakeview, Texas	Graduated from Baylor University	Received a teaching certificate from University of Texas, Austin	Elected Travis County Commissioner

Political Pioneer

[3]   In the 1950s, Richards began volunteering for political campaigns and causes dedicated to the Civil Rights movement and economic justice. After her children were grown, she decided to take a new step. First, she won the 1976 Travis County Commissioner election. Then, she was elected to two terms as state treasurer. She was only the second woman to hold the position. In 1991, Richards succeeded in another challenge and was elected the 45th Governor of Texas. In four years, she improved the state's economy and public education. But her personal achievement was appointing, or hiring, many women and minorities. Richards would not win the re-election for governor, losing to future president George W. Bush.

Death and Legacy

[4]   After years of service, Richards died on September 13, 2006. But her legacy continues. She co-authored memoirs, including *I'm Not Slowing Down*. In 2013, a one-woman play called *Ann* opened on Broadway to great success. In 2014, the documentary *All About Ann* was released. It showed her as a quick-witted, strong woman.

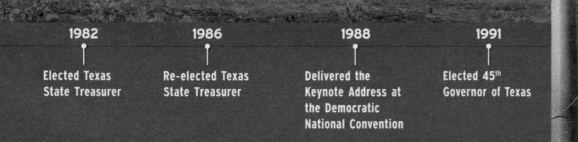

1982	1986	1988	1991	2003	September 13 2006
Elected Texas State Treasurer	Re-elected Texas State Treasurer	Delivered the Keynote Address at the Democratic National Convention	Elected 45th Governor of Texas	Co-authored *I'm Not Slowing Down*	Died, age 73

1 What context clue tells you what the word <u>appointing</u> in paragraph 3 means?

A during

B succeeding

C hiring

D losing

2 Which sentence expresses the author's point of view?

F *Richards' lifelong pursuit was filled with passion and energy.*

G *She graduated from high school in 1950.*

H *She was only the second woman to hold the position.*

J *After years of service, Richards died on September 13, 2006.*

3 According to the timeline, after Richards was elected Travis County Commissioner, she —

A graduated from Baylor University.

B was elected Texas State Treasurer.

C was elected 45th Governor of Texas.

D co-authored *I'm Not Slowing Down.*

4 The author organizes the information in sequence by —

F explaining the differences between Richards and other people.

G including Richards' political achievements.

H describing Richards as "quick-witted and strong."

J telling about Richards' life in order, from beginning to end.

> **Quick Tip**
>
> Review the timeline. Circle "Elected Travis County Commissioner." Look at the events that come next on the timeline and compare them to the answer choices.

Read the selection and choose the best answer to each question.

DOG PARK Rules

1.   "Hey, little guy, <u>calm</u> down," I told my six-month-old puppy, Spud. "It's not polite to bark at every dog that gets close to you. I know you are excited. Let's go over to the bench and give you some time to settle down."

2.   Spud's tail fell, his droopy eyes looking at me, confused. I sat on the bench and patted his soft white and tan head.

3.   Of course Spud felt excited. Today was his first time at the dog park. It brought back memories about my first time going to the dog park with Mom many years ago. We had brought our new puppy, Jingles . . .

4.   "It's okay, Jingles," Mom said. "But remember, it's not polite to bark at every dog you see."

5.   Then she turned to me. "Mike, we must follow the rules. So Rule #1 is to keep Jingles from barking too much. We want everyone to enjoy the dog park."

6.   I felt sorry for Jingles. He was just barking because he was excited and wanted to get to know the other dogs. He liked dogs but had never been around that many at once.

SHOW WHAT YOU LEARNED

7   As Mom continued telling us the rules of the dog park, Jingles started scratching at his collar. At home, we take his collar off, so he can be more comfortable. I was just loosening the collar when Mom stopped me.

8   "Oh no," she said. "Rule #2, collars and ID tags must stay on at all times. If Jingles gets lost, people will know who his owner is."

9   "Mom, you said the dog park was fun. Jingles can't do anything!"

10   "It is fun, but we must follow the rules."

11   Just then, Jingles started barking. He spotted a rabbit outside of the dog park. At that moment, someone was leaving the park and the gate was open long enough for Jingles to run out.

12   "Jingles, stop!" I screamed. But Jingles kept running. He chased the rabbit around an oak tree, under benches, and in between people's legs. Finally, the rabbit escaped down a hole.

     Jingles started digging the hole deeper. "Stop, Jingles!" I yelled, as I approached the hole. Grabbing Jingles by the collar, we walked back to the dog park.

13   Mom greeted us at the gate and said, "Rule #3, make sure you open and close the gate quickly so dogs will not get out!"

14   Spud licked my hand and jolted me back to the present. "Okay, Spud, now that we're experts on dog park rules, we can play ball as long as you want." I smiled knowing that Spud and I will have many fun times at the dog park.

1 In paragraph 1, an antonym for the word <u>calm</u> is —

A quiet

B peaceful

C excited

D still

2 From which point of view is the story written?

F first-person

G second-person

H third-person limited

J third-person omniscient

3 Based on the text, the author's purpose is to entertain because —

A he is trying to convince the audience to do something.

B he is sharing a memorable time in his life.

C he is explaining the rules of dog parks.

D he is giving facts about dog parks.

4 The flashback in the story is when —

F Mike goes to the dog park with Spud.

G Mike tells Spud to calm down.

H Spud was barking at other dogs.

J Mike remembers his first time at a dog park with Jingles.

Quick Tip

If you are not sure what the question is asking, you can underline or circle details in the question. Then reread the text to find the answer.

COMPARING GENRES

- In the **Literature Anthology,** reread the expository text "Partaking in Public Service" on pages 192–195, and the biography "Delivering Justice" on pages 196–213.

- Use the Venn diagram below to show how the two genres are both alike and different.

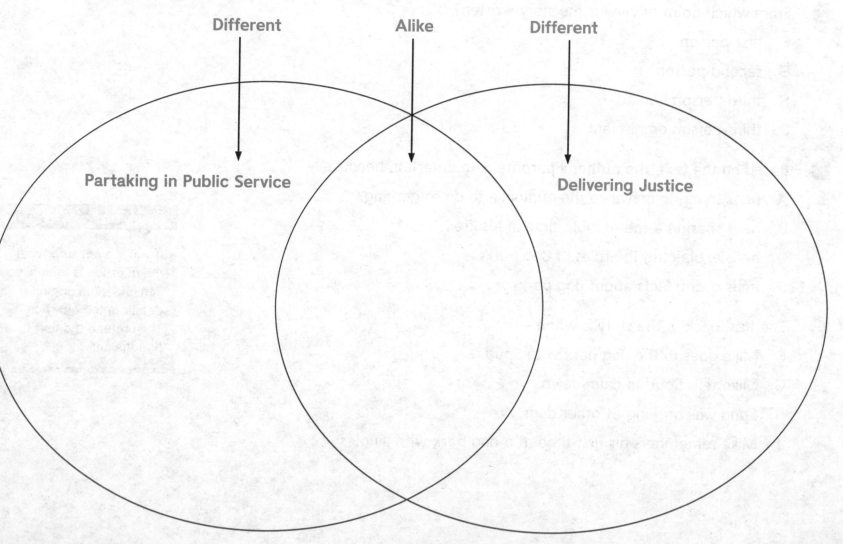

Different   Alike   Different

Partaking in Public Service

Delivering Justice

GREEK ROOTS

COLLABORATE

Knowing Greek roots can help you figure out the meanings of unfamiliar words. You can check the meanings of **Greek roots** in a dictionary.

- Use a print or online dictionary to check the meanings and pronunciations of the Greek roots below.

- Look for words that have these roots.

- Write the definition and example words on the lines.

auto -

Definition: _____

_____

Example words: _____

_____

-meter

Definition: _____

_____

Example words: _____

_____

DRAW A MAP

COLLABORATE

The purpose of a state product map is to show pictures of the major crops and products produced in the state. A product map is a good way to present and discuss information.

- Research major crops, animals raised, or industries in your state.

- Create a map of your state showing pictures of the products. Make a map key to show what the pictures represent. Include a compass rose.

- Share your map with the rest of the class.

List the products you learned about: _____

WATCH A PRIMARY SOURCE VIDEO

COLLABORATE

A primary source is an original source. Primary sources can include documents, diaries, videos, and letters.

- Watch a video about someone who works in an industry in your state. For example, watch an interview with a farmer or an energy worker.

- As you watch, take notes about what you learned.

Write your answers below.

The video I watched was about _____

Describe what you learned about the topic. _____

_____

_____

WRITE DIRECTIONS FOR GROWING A PLANT

COLLABORATE

Directions explain to readers how to do something step by step. Directions can be written in sentences, or as a numbered list.

- Research how to grow a plant in your home or classroom.

- Then write directions for how to grow a plant from a seed.

- Draw a picture of each step and label it.

- Include information about how much sunlight and water is needed.

- Have your partner restate the directions. Then you restate the directions.

Write the directions for growing a plant below.

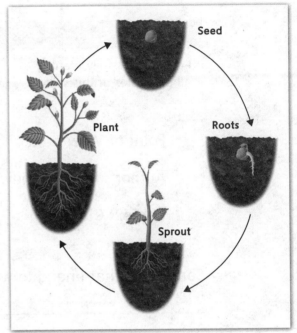

_____

_____

_____

_____

_____

TRACK YOUR PROGRESS

WHAT DID YOU LEARN?

Use the rubric to evaluate yourself on the skills that you learned in this unit. Write your scores in the boxes below.

4	3	2	1
I can successfully identify all examples of this skill.	I can identify most examples of this skill.	I can identify a few examples of this skill.	I need to work on this skill more.

☐ Point of View

☐ Author's Point of View

☐ Context Clues

☐ Synonyms and Antonyms

☐ Greek Roots

Something that I need to work more on is _____ because

_____

_____

_____

Text to Self Think back over the texts that you have read in this unit. Choose one text and write a short paragraph explaining a personal connection that you have made to the text.

I made a personal connection to _____ because _____

_____

_____

Present Your Work

Discuss how you will present your slide show about a main agricultural crop in your state. Use the Presenting Checklist as you practice. Discuss the sentence starters below and write your answers.

An interesting fact that I learned about the major agricultural crop in my state is _____

_____

_____

I would like to know more about _____

_____

_____

_____

Quick Tip

As you present your slide show, read the text on each slide. Speak clearly and loudly.

If there is a diagram, read the title and describe what the diagram shows.

Use these sentence starters.

- *The diagram shows . . .*
- *The different parts of the diagram are . . .*

✓ Presenting Checklist

- ☐ Rehearse your presentation in front of a friend. Ask for feedback.
- ☐ Speak with appropriate rate and expression.
- ☐ Emphasize important information.
- ☐ Make eye contact with the people in the audience.
- ☐ Listen carefully to questions from the audience.

Talk About It

The justice system is an example of government at work. Judges are appointed by elected officials or elected by the voters. Juries are made up of citizens who listen to the evidence presented by both sides. In the web below, write words that give other examples of the roles that government plays.

Government

David Frazier/The Image Bank/Getty Images

 Go online to **my.mheducation.com** and read the "Vote for Me" Blast. Think about how government works. Why is voting important? Then blast back your response.

TAKE NOTES

Establish a purpose for reading. When you are reading for information, identify how the author organizes the information. Preview the text and write your purpose for reading.

_____

_____

_____

As you read, make note of:

Interesting Words _____

_____

_____

_____

Key Details _____

_____

_____

_____

_____

_____

A WORLD WITHOUT RULES

CLOSED

Essential Question

?

Why do we need government?

Read how government and laws help to protect us every day.

You may sometimes wonder if rules were made to keep you from having fun and to tell you what to do. But what if we had no rules at all? Nobody would tell you what to do ever again! Sounds great, right? Well, let's see what it's like to inhabit a world without rules. You just might change your mind!

A Strange Morning

Let's start at home. Your alarm clock goes off. Why hurry? Without rules you don't have to go to school. **Eventually** you wander downstairs and find your little brother eating cookies in the kitchen. Since there are no rules, you can have cookies for breakfast! But you wonder if you should have something sensible like a bowl of cereal. You reach a **compromise (KOM•pru•mize)** and crumble the cookies over your cereal. In this new world, you will not have to brush your teeth anymore. No one will report you. Of course, the next time you see the dentist, you may have a cavity.

A Community in Confusion

Now, you step outside. You decide to go to the playground because there's no law saying you have to go to school. No crossing guard stands at the corner to help you across the street. Without traffic laws, cars zip by at an alarming speed honking at each other, and there is not a police officer in sight. There is no safe alternate way to cross the street. Besides, once you see the playground, you may decide it is not worth the risk of getting hit by a car. Broken swings dangle from rusty chains. Trash cans overflow with plastic bottles, snack wrappers, and paper bags. A huge tree branch lies across the sliding board. As a result of all state and federal services being gone, nobody is in charge of taking care of the playground.

R. G. Roth

FIND TEXT EVIDENCE

Read

Paragraphs 1–3

Cause and Effect

Underline the sentence in paragraph 1 that tells what the effect would be if we had no rules. **Draw a box** around the words in paragraph 3 that tell what causes cars to zip by at an alarming speed.

Ask and Answer Questions

What happens to a playground with no state and federal services?

_____

_____

_____

_____

Reread

Author's Craft

How does the author's use of cause-and-effect text structure help you understand what would happen without rules?

FIND TEXT EVIDENCE 🔍

Read

Paragraphs 1-2

Cause and Effect

Circle the words that tell you why you would not find a place to play soccer.

What is the effect of not having an army?

_____

_____

Latin Roots

The Latin root *commun* means "together." **Underline** the word that contains the root. Write the word.

_____

Reread

Author's Craft

How does the author use headings to organize information?

Now think about trying to do all the other things you love. Want to go to the beach? The lifeguards will not be there to keep you safe. Want to play soccer in the park? Your state and local governments are not around to maintain the parks, so you'll never find a place to play. Feel like eating lunch outside? As a result of pollution, the air quality is so bad that you will probably have to wear a gas mask every day.

Have you ever thought about our country being invaded by another country? Remember, the government runs the army. Without the government, there is no army to protect us if another country decided to take over our country.

Back to Reality

Thankfully, that **version** of our world isn't real. We live in a **democracy** (di•MOK•ruh•see) where we have the **privilege** (PRIV•uh•lij) of voting for the people whom we want to run the country. Our elected government passes **legislation** (lej•is•LAY•shuhn), or laws, meant to help and protect us. If the country outgrows an old law, then the government can pass **amendments** to the law. Community workers such as crossing guards, police officers, and lifeguards all work to keep you safe, while government agencies such as the Environmental Protection Agency have made a **commitment** to inspect the air and water for pollution. And don't forget the armed forces, which were created to protect our nation.

Our government and laws were designed to keep you safe and ensure that you are treated as fairly as everyone else. Without them, the world would be a different place.

Summarize

Use your notes and the headings to orally summarize, or retell, the important events in "A World Without Rules."

FIND TEXT EVIDENCE 🔍

Read

Paragraphs 3-4

Headings/Pronunciations

Why is "Back to Reality" a good heading for this section?

_____

_____

Draw a box around the words that have pronunciations. Which of these words has the fewest syllables?

_____

Evaluate Information

Use the information in the text to tell why government agencies are important.

Reread

Author's Craft

How does the author use reasons and evidence to show that we need rules?

R. G. Roth

Vocabulary

Use the example sentences to talk with a partner about each word. Then answer the questions.

amendments

We made **amendments**, or changes, to the class rules.

Why do we need amendments?

_____

_____

commitment

I made a **commitment** to babysit for my little brother today.

What is a commitment you have made?

_____

compromise

Sam and his dad agreed to **compromise** on when Sam should walk the dog.

Describe a time when you had to compromise.

_____

_____

democracy

In a **democracy**, the government is run by the people.

Why is voting an important right in a democracy?

_____

_____

eventually

The rain **eventually** stopped and the sun came out.

What job do you eventually want to have?

_____

_____

Build Your Word List Choose one of the interesting words you noted on page 100. Use a print or digital dictionary to look up the word's meaning. Then review how many syllables the word has and how it is pronounced.

legislation

Congress passes **legislation** to protect and help citizens.

Why might we need new legislation?

_____

_____

privilege

I had the **privilege** of running for class president.

What is a privilege you wish you had?

_____

_____

_____

version

I like the old **version** of this movie better than the new one.

What are some things that have different versions?

_____

_____

Latin Roots

Knowing Latin roots can help you figure out the meanings of unfamiliar words. Look for these Latin roots as you reread "A World Without Rules."

dent = tooth   port = carry

spect = look   commun = together

🔍 FIND TEXT EVIDENCE

In the third paragraph on page 101, I see the word alternate. *The Latin root* alter *means "other." This will help me figure out what* alternate *means.*

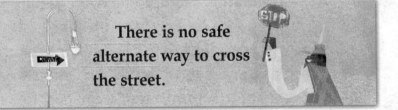

There is no safe alternate way to cross the street.

Your Turn Use Latin roots and context clues to figure out the meanings of these words.

dentist, page 101 _____

_____

report, page 101 _____

_____

inspect, page 102 _____

Ask and Answer Questions

As you read, you may come across new facts and ideas. Stop and ask yourself questions to help you understand and remember the information. Then read the text closely to find the answers.

🔍 FIND TEXT EVIDENCE

When you first read the "Back to Reality" section in "A World Without Rules," you might have asked yourself what role the Environmental Protection Agency has in keeping people safe.

Page 102

> Community workers such as crossing guards, police officers, and lifeguards all work to keep you safe, while government agencies such as the Environmental Protection Agency have made a **commitment** to inspect the air and water for pollution.

As I read on, I found the answer to my question. The Environmental Protection Agency's role is to inspect our air and water and make sure that they are clean.

Your Turn Read "Back to Reality" and ask a question about government. Find the answer and write it here.

_____

_____

_____

Quick Tip

As you read a paragraph, underline any ideas on the topic that are not clear to you. Then ask yourself a question about the information you don't understand. Read on to find the answer.

Headings and Pronunciations

"A World Without Rules" is narrative nonfiction.

Narrative nonfiction

- tells a factual story in an interesting way
- may express the author's opinion about the subject
- presents facts and includes text features

FIND TEXT EVIDENCE

"A World Without Rules" is narrative nonfiction. The author describes a situation and includes text features. The author also expresses an opinion and supports it with facts and examples.

Page 101

You may sometimes wonder if rules were made to keep you from having fun and to tell you what to do. But what if we had no rules at all? Nobody would tell you what to do ever again! Sounds great, right? Well, let's see what it's like to inhabit a world without rules. You just might change your mind!

A Strange Morning

Let's start at home. Your alarm clock goes off. Why hurry? Without rules you don't have to go to school. **Eventually** you wander downstairs and find your little brother eating cookies in the kitchen. Since there are no rules, you can have cookies for breakfast! But you wonder if you should have something sensible like a bowl of cereal. You reach a **compromise (KOM•pru•mize)** and crumble the cookies over your cereal. In this new world, you will not have to brush your teeth anymore. No one will report you. Of course, the next time you see the dentist, you may have a cavity.

A Community in Confusion

Now, you step outside. You decide to go to the playground because there's no law saying you have to go to school. No crossing guard stands at the corner to help you across the street. Without traffic laws, cars zip by at an alarming speed honking at each other, and there is not a police officer in sight. There is no safe alternate way to cross the street. Besides, once you see the playground, you may decide it is not worth the risk of getting hit by a car. Broken swings dangle from rusty chains. Trash cans overflow with plastic bottles, snack wrappers, and paper bags. A huge tree branch lies across the sliding board. As a result of all state and federal services being gone, nobody is in charge of taking care of the playground.

Headings Headings tell you what the section is mostly about.

Pronunciations Pronunciations show how to sound out unfamiliar words.

Your Turn How does the author use headings to keep the reader interested?

_____

_____

_____

Cause and Effect

Authors use text structure to organize the information in a nonfiction text. **Cause and effect** is one kind of text structure. A cause is why something happens. An effect is what happens. Signal words such as *because, so, since,* and *as a result* can help you identify cause-and-effect relationships.

 FIND TEXT EVIDENCE

When I reread the section "A Strange Morning" on page 101, I will look for causes and effects. I will also look for signal words.

Cause	→	Effect
Without rules	→	You don't have to go to school.
Without rules	→	You can have cookies for breakfast.
You don't have to brush your teeth.	→	You may get a cavity.

 Your Turn Reread the section "A Community in Confusion" on pages 101–102. Identify the causes and effects. List them in the graphic organizer on page 109.

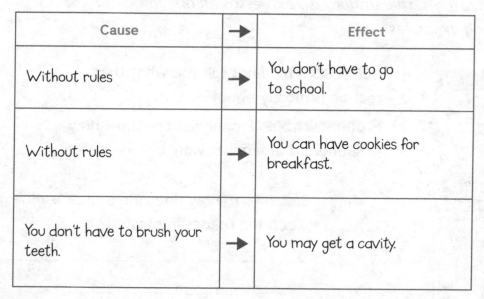

Cause	→	Effect
	→	
	→	
	→	
	→	

Respond to Reading

COLLABORATE

Discuss the prompt below. Think about how the author presents the information. Use your notes, vocabulary words, and graphic organizer.

Why is "A World Without Rules" a good title for this selection?

_____

_____

_____

_____

_____

_____

_____

_____

_____

_____

_____

_____

Skim and Scan

Skimming and scanning will help you when you do research.

Skim means "to read quickly" to get the main idea of a text. To skim, read the title, headings, and the first sentence in each paragraph. Next, look for any italicized or boldfaced words. Then, look at any illustrations, photos, tables, diagrams, and other visuals.

Scan means "to search quickly" for specific information. To scan, you need to know the specific information you are looking for. First, look quickly down the page in search of key words or phrases. Then, look at how the text is divided or organized.

Scan for the name of the governor in the meeting notice. Write it here.

_____

Make a Slideshow With a partner make a multimodal slideshow about the branches of your state government. A slideshow is called multimodal because you can present information in different ways. For example, you can add audio clips, diagrams, and photographs to your slideshow. Discuss how skimming and scanning can help you in your research. Use the questions below to help with your research.

- Who is the head of the Executive branch?
- How many members are in the Legislative branch?
- What courts are included in the Judicial branch?

Use your research to make a diagram of your state government branches for one of your slides. Include labels or captions to describe the functions of each branch.

AIR QUALITY MEETING

Concerned citizens are meeting this week to vote on air-quality limits in our state.

MAKE YOUR VOTE COUNT

Do your part for clean air in the community. Join your fellow citizens at **8 p.m. on Thursday at Town Hall.** Mayor John Ashford and Governor Jane Hamilton are expected to speak before the final vote.

See How They Run

 How does the author help you understand what the Founding Fathers did?

Literature Anthology: pages 270–281

 Talk About It Reread page 273 of the **Literature Anthology**. Turn and talk to your partner about how George Washington and the Founding Fathers created our American government.

Cite Text Evidence What examples show how the Founding Fathers used ideas from Greek and Roman governments? Write text evidence in the chart.

 **Synthesize Information**

Remember, when you synthesize information, you combine information to create a new understanding.

What were the differences between Roman and Greek governments? What were the similarities?

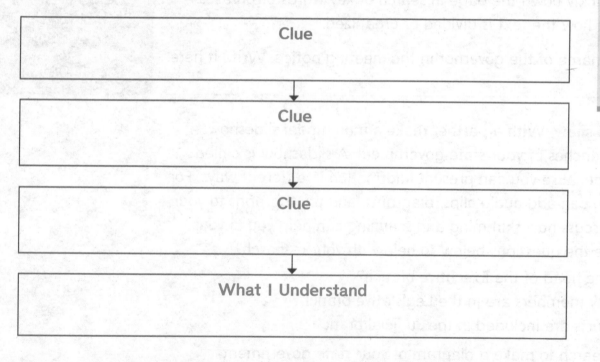

```
Clue
   ↓
Clue
   ↓
Clue
   ↓
What I Understand
```

Write The author helps me understand what the Founding Fathers did by

_____

_____

Why does the author include Ben Franklin's quote in the sidebar?

Talk About It Reread the sidebar on page 274 of the **Literature Anthology**. Turn and talk with a partner about what Ben Franklin said.

Cite Text Evidence What words and phrases help you understand Ben Franklin's message? Write text evidence in the chart.

Text Evidence	Author's Purpose

Write The author includes Ben Franklin's quote to _____

_____

_____

? **Why does the author give specific, real-life examples of kids as leaders?**

Talk About It Reread page 279 of the **Literature Anthology**. Turn to your partner and talk about how Shadia Wood helped her community.

Cite Text Evidence What words and phrases show what Shadia did to help her community? Write text evidence in the chart.

What Shadia Did	How It Helped	Author's Purpose

Write The author gives real-life examples of kids as leaders to _____

_____

_____

nito/Shutterstock.com

Respond to Reading

Discuss the prompt below. Use your own knowledge, your notes, and the graphic organizers to help you.

What is the author's point of view about democracy and our right to vote?

_____

_____

_____

_____

_____

_____

_____

_____

_____

_____

_____

_____

The Birth of American Democracy

Literature Anthology:
pages 284–287

1   Every Fourth of July, Americans celebrate the birthday of the United States. Fireworks and parades remind us that the thirteen colonies declared independence from Great Britain on July 4, 1776. That birthday took place in Philadelphia, Pennsylvania. There, the Second Continental Congress approved the Declaration of Independence. This document formed a new nation, the United States of America. The Declaration is almost like our country's original birthday card.

Our Founding Fathers

2   Five men, including John Adams, Thomas Jefferson, and Benjamin Franklin, wrote the Declaration of Independence. Jefferson wrote the first draft. His famous words sum up a basic American belief—"all men are created equal."

Reread paragraph 1. **Underline** two details that explain why the Fourth of July is called America's birthday.

COLLABORATE

Talk with a partner about how the author describes the Declaration of Independence. **Draw a circle** around the text evidence.

In paragraph 2, **make a checkmark** next to the line that tells what Thomas Jefferson believed. Write it here:

_____

_____

3   The men who signed the Declaration are called the Founding Fathers of our country. Signing the Declaration put the founders' lives in danger. They knew that their signatures made them traitors to Great Britain. They also knew that, if the colonies won the war, their names would go down in history.

4   Led by General George Washington, the colonists fought passionately for their freedom. After a long, bloody war, the British surrendered in 1781, and a peace treaty was signed in 1783. Our new nation was still a work in progress, however. Americans disagreed about how much power a federal, or central, government should have. Given that they had just won freedom from a powerful British king, Americans did not want their government to have too much power.

Reread paragraph 3. **Underline** the details that tell you how the Declaration of Independence was both risky and positive for the Founding Fathers. Write it here:

_____

_____

_____

COLLABORATE

Reread paragraph 4. Talk with a partner about how the author shows how the colonists felt about freedom. **Circle** the text evidence.

? **Why is "The Birth of American Democracy" a good title for this selection?**

Talk About It Reread the excerpts on pages 116 and 117. Talk about why the Fourth of July is such an important holiday.

Cite Text Evidence What words and phrases show how our government was created? Write text evidence in the chart. Explain the author's purpose for presenting these details.

Quick Tip

Look for specific details or ideas in the text that tell you what happened on July 4, 1776. The details or ideas are important to the meaning of the author's purpose.

Text Evidence	Author's Purpose

Write "The Birth of American Democracy" is a good title because _____

_____

_____

Homophones and Homographs

Readers to Writers

When you write, make sure to use the correct spelling of any words that are homophones. For example, these homophones are frequently confused: *their, there, they're.* Write a sentence for each homophone. Explain why you used that homophone.

Homophones are two words that *sound* the same but are spelled differently and have different meanings.

- Examples: Pull the thread <u>through</u> the needle. He <u>threw</u> the ball.

Homographs are words that are *spelled* the same but have different meanings and origins. Use context clues to figure out the meanings of homographs.

- Examples: The <u>wind</u> blows. <u>Wind</u> the string around your finger.

 FIND TEXT EVIDENCE

On page 117 in paragraph 3, the author uses the homophone *their* and the homograph *lives*. The context of each sentence can help readers understand the word's meaning and how to pronounce it.

> Signing the Declaration put the founders' lives in danger. They knew that their signatures made them traitors to Great Britain.

Your Turn Reread the first paragraph on page 116.

- Find a word that can be a homograph and write its two meanings. ____

  _____

- What word also has a homophone? Write the word and its homophone. _____

  _____

Text Connections

? **What did you learn about government from** *See How They Run* **and "The Birth of American Democracy"? How does government protect people's rights?**

Talk About It Tarriers are people who waste time. In the song, the tarriers are the railroad workers who can't work quickly enough to meet the foreman's demands. Read the lyrics. Talk with a partner about how government can help to protect Jim Goff.

Cite Text Evidence **Circle** words and phrases in the lyrics that show how the songwriter feels about Jerry McCann. **Underline** what Jerry McCann says.

Write The songwriter and authors show how

government is important because _____

_____

_____

_____

Datacraft Co Ltd/Getty Images

from Drill, Ye Tarriers

Now, our new foreman was Jerry
    McCann,
You can bet that he was sure a
    blame mean man,
Last week a premature blast went off,
And a mile in the air went big Jim Goff,
Now, next time payday come around,
Jim Goff a dollar short was found,
When asked what for, came this reply,
"You were docked for the time you were
    up in the sky!"

Present Your Work

COLLABORATE

Discuss how you will present your multimodal slideshow to the class. You may want to post it on a digital bulletin board. Use the checklist as you rehearse your presentation, and listen carefully to your classmates' questions.

Our State Government

Legislature

General Assembly

Judicial

Courts

Executive

Governor

Discuss the sentence starters below and write your answers.

An interesting fact that I learned about our state government is _____

_____

_____

I would like to know more about _____

_____

Tech Tip

A slideshow allows you to organize your text and visuals. Too much information on other slides, however, encourages people to read, not listen to you. So just put a sentence or two on each slide, like an outline, then present most of the information orally.

Presenting Checklist

- [ ] Rehearse your presentation in front of a friend. Ask for feedback.
- [ ] Speak slowly, clearly, and with expression.
- [ ] Point to visuals related to your topic as you present information.
- [ ] Listen carefully to questions from the audience.
- [ ] Use formal language to clarify and answer questions.

Literature Anthology:
pages 270–281

Expert Model

Features of a Narrative Nonfiction Essay

A narrative nonfiction essay is written in the form of a story. It informs readers about a real subject by presenting information in an interesting way. A narrative nonfiction essay

- tells about real people and events

- may include the writer's feelings and opinions

- presents facts and includes text features

Word Wise

The first sentence on page 278 is: *Bugging your parents is a good first step.* This sentence is an example of author Susan E. Goodman's use of informal language. Her use of informal language contributes to the humorous voice in her writing.

Analyze an Expert Model Studying narrative nonfiction texts will help you learn how to write a narrative nonfiction essay. Reread page 279 of *See How They Run* in the **Literature Anthology**. Write your answers below.

What anecdote is the author telling? _____

_____

_____

_____

Which detail in the paragraph shows the author's opinion? _____

_____

_____

Plan: Choose Your Topic

Brainstorm With a partner or a small group, brainstorm as many people as possible who have been important figures in your state government since it first became a state.

_____

_____

_____

Writing Prompt Write a narrative nonfiction essay about one of the historical figures on your list. Explain how that person contributed to your state government.

I will write about _____

Purpose and Audience An **author's purpose** is his or her main reason for writing. Underline your purpose for writing a narrative nonfiction essay.

   to inform, or teach   to persuade, or convince   to entertain

Think about the audience for your essay. Who will read it?

My audience will be _____.

Plan In your writer's notebook, make a cause-and-effect chart to plan your essay about an important state historical figure.

Quick Tip

To help you plan for a certain audience, ask yourself:

• What do they already know about my topic?

• What more do they need to know?

• What opinions do they have?

• Would they be more interested if I used formal or informal language?

Cause	→	Effect
	→	
	→	
	→	
	→	

Plan: Cause-and-Effect Text Structure

What Happened? Why Did It Happen? Things don't just happen; people or things make them happen. The person or thing is the **cause**; what happens is the **effect**. As you research and plan your narrative about a historical figure in your state government, answer these questions:

- What effect did he or she have on your state government?

- What did he or she do to cause change?

- How do those changes affect your life today?

List two causes and effects you could use in your narrative.

1 _____

_____

2 _____

_____

 Take Notes As you take notes on your topic, paraphrase information by putting it into your own words. When you have finished taking notes, use your cause-and-effect chart to organize the information you will use in your essay. Include only the most important details to keep your chart entries brief.

Draft

Relevant Details Authors use details to support the main idea of their writing. All the details should relate to the subject. In the example below from the Differentiated Genre Passage "Get Involved," the author sticks to one point—creating a petition.

> If you want to get others involved, you can create a petition. A petition is a document asking for change. The word *petition* comes from the Latin root *petere*, which means to "see or request." Take your petition around to everyone you know and ask them to sign it. Then send it to your local government to show them that a lot of people feel the same way you do.

Quick Tip

How do you know if a detail is relevant? It has to relate to the subject. Read these sentences:

John became governor at age 28. He served for two terms. My sister was a nurse before she was 28. John went on to become a U.S. Senator.

Which sentence is not relevant? The third sentence is not relevant because it has nothing to do with John!

Now use the above paragraph as a model to write the main idea of your essay and a relevant detail.

_____

_____

_____

_____

_____

Write a Draft Use your cause-and-effect chart to help you write your draft in your writer's notebook. Don't forget that you are telling a real-life story, so think about how you can use informal language to make it more interesting.

Revise

Transitions Effective writers make sure that they use transitions to link their ideas together. Some transition words are: *however, but, afterward, because*. Read the paragraph below. Then revise it so the cause-and-effect ideas are logically linked together.

> He became governor. Millions of people voted for him.
>
> A governor can only serve two terms. He went back to teaching.

_____

_____

_____

_____

_____

 Revision Revise your draft, and check that you present relevant facts with transitions. Make sure that you have told the facts in a narrative form, which might include some opinions about your subject.

Rich Legg/E+/Getty Images

Grammar Connections

As you revise your draft, check that any quotations have the correct punctuation marks. Remember to use quotation marks before and after the exact words someone says or writes. Put a period, question mark, or exclamation mark inside the quotation marks when it is part of the quotation, as in: *He said, "All men are created equal."*

Peer Conferences

COLLABORATE

Review a Draft Listen carefully as a partner reads his or her work aloud. Take notes about what you liked and what was difficult to follow. Begin by telling what you liked about the draft. Ask questions that will help the writer think more about the writing. Make suggestions that you think will make the writing more focused and coherent. Use these sentence starters.

I enjoyed the way you started your piece because . . .

Another relevant detail you might add is . . .

I don't understand this transition. Can you explain why . . . ?

Partner Feedback After your partner gives you feedback on your draft, write one of the suggestions that you will use in your revision. Refer to the rubric on page 129 as you give feedback.

Based on my partner's feedback, I will _____

_____

After you finish giving each other feedback, reflect on the peer conference. What was helpful? What might you do differently next time?

Revision As you revise your draft, use the Revising Checklist to help you figure out what ideas you may need to add, delete, combine, or rearrange. Remember to use the rubric on page 129 to help with your revision.

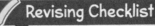
Revising Checklist

- [ ] Does my writing fit my purpose and audience?
- [ ] Did I use a consistent tone and voice as the narrator?
- [ ] Did I use transition words to combine ideas?
- [ ] Did I improve sentence structure by combining some simple sentences into compound sentences?
- [ ] Did I rearrange some sentences to make them clearer?

┌─ **Digital Tools** ─────────────────────────
For more information on peer conferencing, watch the "Peer Conferencing" (Collaborative Conversations) video.
Go to **my.mheducation.com**.
└──

Edit and Proofread

When you **edit** and **proofread** your writing, you look for and correct mistakes in spelling, punctuation, capitalization, and grammar. Reading through a revised draft multiple times can help you make sure you're catching any errors. Use the checklist below to edit your sentences.

✓ Editing Checklist

☐ Do all sentences begin with a capital letter and end with a punctuation mark?

☐ Do all the sentences have subjects and predicates?

☐ Are any headings capitalized and boldfaced?

☐ Are possessive nouns used correctly?

☐ Are words that have homophones used correctly?

☐ Are all other words spelled correctly?

Grammar Connections

When you proofread your essay, you may need to double-check any word that has a homophone. For example, you might use *hear* when you mean *here*, *rain* when you mean *reign*, *its* when you mean *it's*, or *your* when you mean *you're*.

List two mistakes you found as you proofread your essay.

1 _____

_____

2 _____

_____

Publish, Present, and Evaluate

Publishing When you **publish** your writing, you create a clean, neat final copy that is free of mistakes. As you write your final draft, be sure to write legibly in cursive. Check that you are holding your pencil or pen correctly between your forefinger and thumb.

Presentation When you are ready to **present** your work, rehearse your presentation. Use the Presenting Checklist to help you.

Evaluate After you publish your writing, use the rubric below to **evaluate** your writing.

☐ Stand up straight.

☐ Look at the audience.

☐ Use a friendly, informal tone.

☐ Speak clearly and loud enough for everyone to hear you.

☐ Answer questions from the audience thoughtfully.

What did you do successfully? _____

_____

What needs more work? _____

_____

4	3	2	1
• told in engaging, narrative style with clear central idea	• told in narrative style with central idea	• told in narrative style with unclear central idea	• told in narrative style but with no central idea
• includes only relevant facts	• includes mostly relevant facts	• includes irrelevant facts	• lacks facts
• Includes author's feelings and opinions	• includes author's feelings	• unclear author's feelings or opinions	• no author's feelings or opinions
• few if any errors in grammar or spelling	• some errors, but not enough to affect meaning	• frequent errors that might confuse the reader	• many errors make it difficult to follow

Talk About It

For some people, new inventions and advanced technology provide a way to fulfill their dreams. The man in the photo is able to compete in the Paralympics with an artificial leg, which allows him to run long distances.

In the chart, describe the effect inventions and technology have on your life. Then, talk with your partner about an invention you would like to design. Describe how it would change your life.

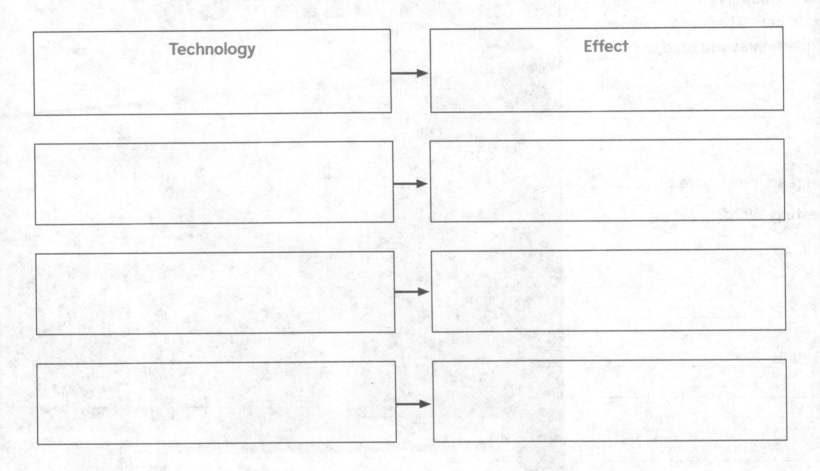

Technology	Effect

Go online to **my.mheducation.com** and read the "Technology Today" Blast. Think about how technology has affected our everyday lives. Then blast back your response.

TAKE NOTES

To help you understand what you will be reading, preview the text and ask a question about the title and illustrations. Write your question here. Then try to answer your question as you read.

_____

_____

_____

As you read, make note of:

Interesting Words _____

_____

_____

_____

Key Details _____

_____

_____

_____

_____

_____

_____

_____

_____

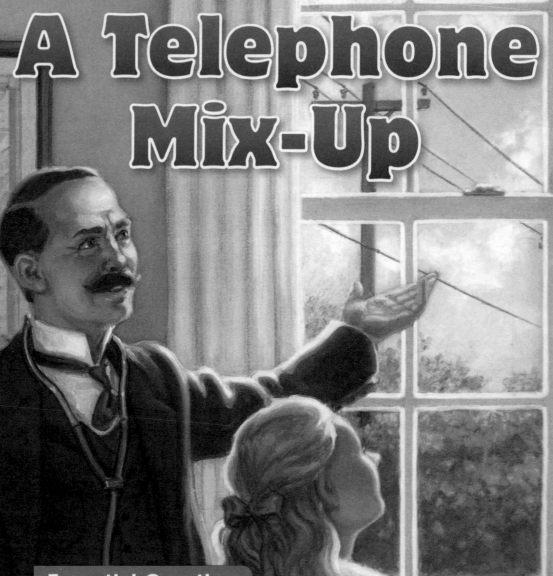

A Telephone Mix-Up

Essential Question

 How do inventions and technology affect your life?

Read how a telephone brings change to the lives of Meg and her father.

"By tomorrow afternoon there will be eight telephones right here in Centerburg, Ohio, and one of them will be ours!" Dr. Ericksen said to his daughter, Meg. "I predict that before this **decade** is over, in just another five years, there could be a hundred! That's how fast I foresee this **technology** will spread! When people need help, they'll call me on the telephone. Envision how many lives it will save! Picture all the amazing benefits!"

Meg realized that not everyone thought the telephone was an **engineering** marvel. She had heard people say that telephones were a useless invention. A few others felt the newfangled machine would open up a Pandora's box of troubles, causing people to stop visiting each other and writing letters.

Despite the concerns of some people, progress marched on. Just weeks earlier, Centerburg's first telephone had been installed in Mr. Kane's general store, another was put in at the hotel, and yet another at the newspaper office. Mrs. Kane was the town's first switchboard operator, **directing** incoming calls to the correct lines.

The next morning, Meg wrote "October 9, 1905" on the top of her slate with chalk while she **squirmed** in her seat, wishing that the long school day was over.

HISTORICAL FICTION

FIND TEXT EVIDENCE

Read

Paragraphs 1–4
Point of View

Circle the pronouns that tell you the story is told from the third-person point of view.

Paragraphs 1–4
Setting

Draw a box around the details that tell the setting of the story.

Paragraphs 2–4
Make Predictions

Underline the words that tell how other people feel about the telephone. Predict how they will react to it in a year.

_____

_____

_____

Reread

Author's Craft

How does the author's use of the word *squirmed* help you understand how Meg is feeling?

FIND TEXT EVIDENCE 🔍

Read

Paragraphs 1–2
Point of View

Draw a box around how Meg thinks the telephone will affect her life.

Synonyms

Underline the phrase that is a synonym for the word *scouted*. Write the phrase on the line.

Paragraphs 3–8
Dialogue

Circle the dialogue that tells you the telephone was a new invention that still had problems.

Reread

Author's Craft

How does the author use dialogue to help you understand the relationship between Meg and her father?

Walking home that afternoon, Meg **scouted** the street, looking for the tall wooden poles that were going up weekly. Thick wire linked one pole to another, and Meg imagined how each wire would carry the words of friends and neighbors, their conversations zipping over the lines bringing news, birthday wishes, and party invitations.

As Meg hurried into the house, she let the screen door slam shut behind her. There on the wall was the **gleaming** wooden telephone box with its heavy black receiver on a hook. Her father was smiling broadly while **tinkering** with the shiny brass bells on top. "Isn't it a beauty?" he asked. "Have you ever seen such magnificence?"

Suddenly the telephone jangled loudly, causing both Ericksens to jump.

Meg laughed as her father picked up the receiver and shouted, "Yes, hello, this is the doctor!"

"Again please, Mrs. Kane! There's too much static!" Dr. Ericksen shouted. "I didn't get the first part. Bad cough? Turner farm?"

"Can I go, Father?" Meg asked as Dr. Ericksen returned the receiver to the hook.

"Absolutely," he said, grabbing his medical kit and heading outside where his horse and buggy waited.

When they got to the farm, they found Mr. Turner walking toward the barn.

"Jake, I got here as quick as I could," Dr. Ericksen said. "Is it Mrs. Turner? Little Emma?"

"You?" Jake Turner looked confused, but he gestured them toward the barn.

There they found a baby goat curled near its mother. The baby snorted, coughed, and looked miserable.

"Jake, I'm no vet!" said Dr. Ericksen. "You need Dr. Kerrigan."

"I was wondering why you showed up instead. I reckon there was a mix-up."

"Apparently so," Dr. Ericksen laughed. "When I get back, I'll send Dr. Kerrigan."

As years passed, the telephone proved to be very useful to the town of Centerburg, but there was always the occasional mix-up. It became common among the Ericksens to refer to a missed communication as "another sick goat."

Summarize

Use your notes to orally summarize the important events in "A Telephone Mix-Up."

FIND TEXT EVIDENCE 🔍

Read

Paragraphs 1–4
Point of View
Underline the feeling that Mr. Turner has when he sees Dr. Ericksen.

Paragraphs 5–7
Make Inferences
Circle how the telephone affected Centerburg. What can you infer about the kinds of mix-ups the town experienced?

_____

_____

_____

_____

Reread
Author's Craft

What effect does the historical setting have on the plot?

Vocabulary

Use the example sentences to talk with a partner about each word. Then answer the questions.

decade

Rosa's family celebrated a **decade** of living in their home.

What will you be doing in a decade?

_____

_____

directing

Two police officers were **directing** traffic.

If you were a crossing guard, what would you be directing students to do?

_____

_____

engineering

I think the beautiful Golden Gate Bridge is an amazing example of **engineering**.

What is another amazing example of engineering?

_____

_____

gleaming

The **gleaming** sun warmed the swimmers at the park.

What is an antonym for _gleaming_?

_____

_____

scouted

They used binoculars as they **scouted** the best place to find birds.

What have you scouted in the park?

_____

_____

Build Your Word List Choose an interesting word you noted on page 132 and look up the word's pronunciation and definition in a print or digital dictionary. Write the meaning in your writer's notebook and list one synonym for the word.

squirmed

The kitten wiggled and **squirmed** in the girl's arms.

Why might the kitten have squirmed?

_____

_____

technology

In the early 1900s, the telephone was considered new **technology**.

What are some examples of new technology in this century?

_____

_____

tinkering

Mrs. Lan likes **tinkering** with broken bikes.

What is a synonym for _tinkering_?

_____

_____

Synonyms

If a word is unfamiliar to you as you read, it might help to keep reading. Sometimes the author uses another word or phrase nearby that is close in meaning to the unfamiliar word. Words that have the same or similar meanings are **synonyms**.

🔍 FIND TEXT EVIDENCE

As I read the first paragraph of "The Telephone Mix-Up" on page 133, I wasn't sure what the word envision _meant. Then the word_ picture _in the next sentence helped me figure out the meaning._

Envision how many lives it will save! Picture all the amazing benefits!

Your Turn Use synonyms and other context clues to find the meanings of the following words in "A Telephone Mix-Up." Write a synonym and example sentence for each word.

foresee, page 133 _____

_____

magnificence, page 134 _____

_____

Make Predictions

When you read, think about the genre and use text clues from the story to help you make predictions about what will happen next. As you continue to read, you can confirm or revise your predictions.

🔍 FIND TEXT EVIDENCE

How did you predict the people of Centerburg would react to the telephone? What helped you to confirm your prediction? Reread page 133 of "A Telephone Mix-Up."

Page 133

Despite the concerns of some people, progress marched on. Just weeks earlier, Centerburg's first telephone had been installed in Mr. Kane's general store, another was put in at the hotel, and yet another at the newspaper office. Mrs. Kane was the town's first switchboard operator, directing incoming calls to the correct lines.

The next morning, Meg wrote "October 9, 1905" on the top of her slate with chalk while she squirmed in her seat, wishing that the long school day was over.

I had predicted that people in Centerburg would get used to the telephone even though some people would not like the idea of it. Evidence in the paragraph confirmed my prediction.

 Your Turn What text clues did you find that helped you predict that the phone would cause a mix-up? As you read, remember to use the strategy Make Predictions.

_____

_____

Quick Tip

Making predictions about a text can help you check your comprehension. As you read, look for details that will confirm your predictions.

Setting and Dialogue

Historical fiction tells a story set in the past and is often based on real events. Historical fiction

- has realistic characters, events, and settings
- usually includes dialogue
- tells events in time order

 FIND TEXT EVIDENCE

I can tell that "A Telephone Mix-Up" is historical fiction. A family is getting a telephone at a time in history when telephone service was first made available to many communities. The story has realistic characters, events, and settings, and it includes dialogue.

Page 133

"By tomorrow afternoon there will be eight telephones right here in Centerburg, Ohio, and one of them will be ours!" Dr. Ericksen said to his daughter, Meg. "I predict that before this **decade** is over, in just another five years, there could be a hundred! That's how fast I foresee this **technology** will spread! When people need help, they'll call me on the telephone. Envision how many lives it will save! Picture all the amazing benefits!"

Meg realized that not everyone thought the telephone was an **engineering** marvel. She had heard people say that telephones were a useless invention. A few others felt the newfangled machine would open up a Pandora's box of troubles, causing people to stop visiting each other and writing letters.

Despite the concerns of some people, progress marched on. Just weeks earlier, Centerburg's first telephone had been installed in Mr. Kane's general store, another was put in at the hotel, and yet another at the newspaper office. Mrs. Kane was the town's first switchboard operator, **directing** incoming calls to the correct lines.

The next morning, Meg wrote "October 9, 1905" on the top of her slate with chalk while she **squirmed** in her seat, wishing that the long school day was over.

Dialogue

Dialogue is the conversation that takes place between the characters. Quotation marks enclose dialogue.

Setting

Setting is the time and place of the story. The historical setting influences the plot and has an impact on the characters.

 Your Turn Find three examples in the text that show "A Telephone Mix-Up" is historical fiction.

_____

_____

_____

Readers to Writers

Writers use dialogue and setting to develop the events or plot of a story. Think about how the historical setting influences the events of the story. Would the events of "A Telephone Mix-Up" be different if the story was not set in the past? How can you use setting to develop events in your own writing?

Point of View

The narrator's point of view tells how the narrator thinks or feels about characters or events in the story. A story can have a first-person narrator or a third-person narrator.

🔍 FIND TEXT EVIDENCE

When I read page 133 of "A Telephone Mix-Up," I see that the narrator uses the pronouns *she* and *his* when the narrator tells what Meg and her father are thinking. This story has a third-person narrator. I can find details in the story about the narrator's point of view.

Details
The narrator tells us what Meg's father says about the telephone. "Picture all the amazing benefits!"
The narrator states, "Despite the concerns of some people, progress marched on."

↓

Point of View
The narrator thinks the telephone will be a useful invention.

Your Turn Reread "A Telephone Mix-Up." Find other details from the story that tell you the narrator's point of view about Meg's relationship with her father. Use the graphic organizer to list the details.

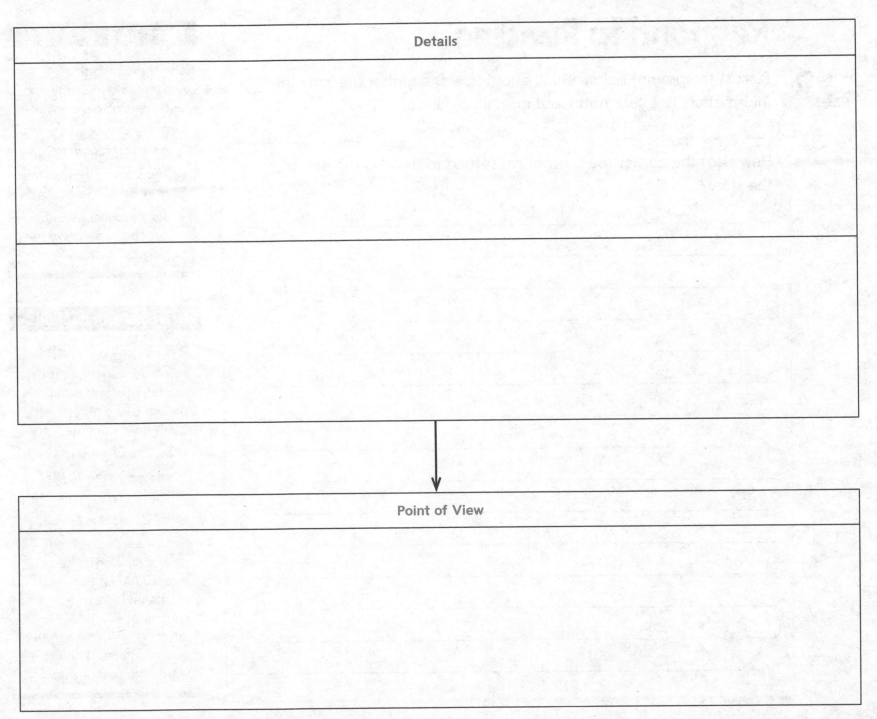

Details

Point of View

Respond to Reading

COLLABORATE

Discuss the prompt below. Think about how the author presents the information. Use your notes and graphic organizer.

How does the author use a historical setting to develop the plot of the story?

_____

_____

_____

_____

_____

_____

_____

_____

_____

_____

_____

_____

_____

_____

Grammar Connections

As you write your response, be sure to use quotation marks around dialogue or direct quotations from the story.

"Absolutely," he said.

"Can I go, Father?" Meg asked.

He said, "Here is Emma."

Remember, a comma goes after words like *said* or *asked* when the quotation follows. A comma goes inside the quotation marks when the quotation comes before words like *said* or *asked*.

Persuasive Language

Persuasive language includes words and phrases that express an opinion or a point of view. This language may also try to convince people to think a certain way or to do something. Here are some examples of persuasive language.

- **Bandwagon:** suggests that many people are doing (or not doing) something, so you should (or should not), too
- **Facts:** gives evidence like percentages or numbers to convince you
- **Endorsement:** asks a famous person or an expert to promote the product or idea

Where have you seen or heard persuasive language? Write your answer.

_____

_____

The image above shows an advertisement. What is the persuasive language trying to convince people to do? Write your answer below.

_____

_____

COLLABORATE

Make a Flyer Create a flyer for a community project. Research a problem and then describe ways your project will improve your community. Tell where and when the event will take place. Remember to use persuasive text. Use these questions to help you plan.

- What facts can you include?
- How will your ideas improve the community?
- Why should others agree with your idea?

Use a computer to add photographs, illustrations, or other graphics to your flyer. After you finish, you will be sharing your work with the class.

Tech Tip

You can find photographs and illustrations online for your flyer. Be sure to use websites that are reliable. Usually, websites for reliable organizations end with *.gov, .edu,* or *.org*. Ask a librarian or other adult for suggestions. Remember to give credit to the websites where you found the images.

PiggyBank/Shutterstock.com

The Moon Over Star

*Literature Anthology:
pages 288–303*

 How does the author help you understand how Gramps feels about the moon landing being shown on television?

 Talk About It Reread **Literature Anthology** page 294. Turn to a partner and discuss Gramps's reaction to the moon landing on television.

Cite Text Evidence What words and phrases show how everyone reacts to Gran's announcement? Write text evidence and explain what it shows.

Response to Gran's Announcement	What This Shows

Write I know how Gramps feels about the moon landing because the author _____

_____

_____

Make Inferences

You can learn about characters by their reactions to events or situations. Think about the historic setting, the moment in time in which the story takes place. What inferences can you make about Gramps from his reaction to the historic moon landing? What is important to him?

Evaluate Information

Rereading the text will help you understand how the setting affects a story. "The Moon Over Star" takes place at an important moment in history. How would the story be different if it did not have this historic setting?

How does the author use words and phrases to help you visualize the mood of that summer night?

Talk About It Reread **Literature Anthology** page 298. Talk with a partner about the author's description of the family's time outside at night. Discuss how that description makes you feel.

Cite Text Evidence What phrases help you picture what that night was like? Write text evidence in the chart.

Evaluate Information

Review the chart with the text evidence of what you visualize. How does the author's use of language (sensory details, figurative language) help the reader visualize the scene? Which evidence do you think most effectively shows the mood of the summer night? Why?

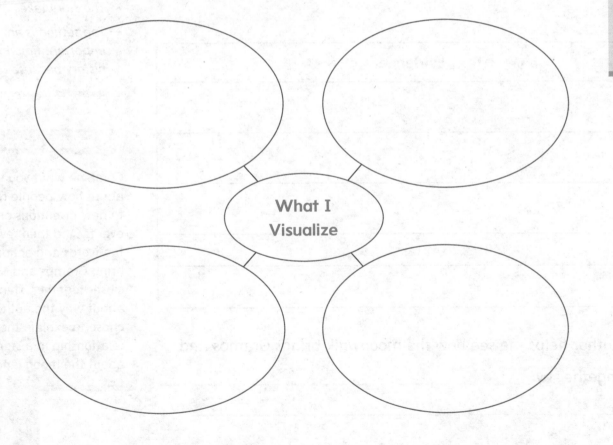

What I Visualize

? How does the moonwalk bring Gramps and Mae closer together?

Talk About It Reread the last paragraph on page 300 of the **Literature Anthology**. Turn to a partner and talk about how Gramps reacts to what the family is watching on television.

Cite Text Evidence What does Gramps say and do? Write text evidence and tell how his actions help you understand how he now feels about the moonwalk.

Text Evidence
What I Understand

Write The author helps me see how the moonwalk brings Gramps and Mae closer together by _____

_____

_____

Respond to Reading

COLLABORATE

Discuss the prompt below and share any questions you have with a partner. Apply your knowledge about how people can change. Use your notes and graphic organizer.

How does the author use a historical event to develop the plot of the story?

_____

_____

_____

_____

_____

_____

_____

_____

_____

_____

Anson_iStock/Getty Images

Star Parties

Literature Anthology:
pages 306–309

Find a Star Party

1   For decades, many national parks and observatories in the United States have held star parties. These are great locations for star parties because they can provide total darkness. . . .

2   Park rangers and astronomers will guide you through the night sky. They will point out and explain the different objects in the sky on that night. There may be sights that are impossible to see where you live. . . .

3   Observatories use powerful technology that astronomers use to do their research. The McDonald Observatory in Texas is located in the Davis Mountains. At the observatory, star parties are held at a telescope park. The park has dome structures with different sized telescopes. One dome has a 24-inch telescope that can be operated by a robot in a remote location—now that's great engineering!

Reread paragraph 1. **Underline** why national parks and observatories are great places for star parties. **Draw a box** around the two things park rangers and astronomers do at star parties. Write them here.

_____

_____

_____

_____

_____

COLLABORATE

Discuss the importance of the McDonald Observatory. **Circle** why it is "great engineering."

What to See

1.   During different times of the year, you will get good views of some of the planets in our solar system. Many star gazers look for the largest planet, Jupiter, with its moons and rings. But if you want to see larger and brighter rings, look for Saturn in the night sky.

2.   There are also numerous constellations. A constellation is a group of stars that form a pattern or image. For example, Orion the Hunter is a constellation that the ancient Greeks thought looked like a hunter with a sword attached to its belt.

3.   At a star party you may get a chance to make a wish under a shooting star, or a meteor. Meteors are not really stars. They are bits of rocks. But they appear in the sky as beautiful streaks of light. When there are many shooting stars in the sky, it is called a meteor shower.

4.   No matter what time of year you go to a star party, you will not be disappointed. There is always something fascinating to see in the night sky.

Reread paragraph 1. **Circle** some of the things people can see in the night sky.

COLLABORATE

Look at the diagram and read the caption. Discuss when you can view the different phases of the Moon. How does the Sun affect the way we see the Moon?

_____

_____

_____

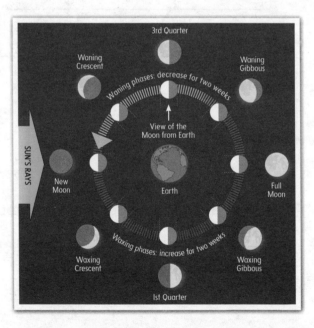

3rd Quarter

Waning Crescent

Waning Gibbous

Waning phases: decrease for two weeks

View of the Moon from Earth

SUN'S RAYS

New Moon

Earth

Full Moon

Waxing phases: increase for two weeks

Waxing Crescent

Waxing Gibbous

1st Quarter

The Moon does not have a light source. When we see the Moon in the night sky, the Sun is shining on it. The

? **What is the author's point of view about star parties?**

COLLABORATE

Talk About It Reread the excerpts on pages 148 and 149. Discuss what you can see and learn from star parties.

Cite Text Evidence What is the author's point of view about what you can see at star parties? Write text evidence in the chart.

Detail	Detail	Detail

Author Point of View

Write The author's point of view about star parties is _____

_____

_____

_____

_____

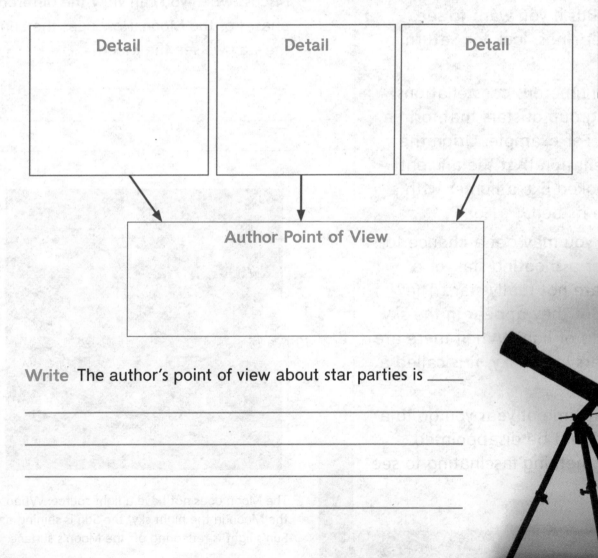

Steve Cole/Getty Images

Sidebars and Insets

Sidebars and insets give readers more information about a topic. Sidebars are boxes found on the side or bottom of a page. Insets are usually small images found near the main text. Both sidebars and insets may provide these features:

- additional information about the topic
- maps, charts, graphs, diagrams
- photographs or illustrations with captions

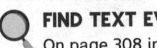 **FIND TEXT EVIDENCE**

On page 308 in the **Literature Anthology** there is an inset about the phases of the Moon. **Circle** the information that tells you how many days pass until the pattern repeats.

> As the Moon orbits Earth, it follows a regular pattern. The pattern repeats every 29 or 30 days. People on Earth see different parts of the Moon as it orbits Earth. The different patterns are called Moon phases.

Your Turn Read the inset "Phases of the Moon" on page 308.

- Why does the author include the inset? _____

_____

- How does the inset help readers better understand the Moon phases?

_____

_____

Text Connections

? **How do the authors of the "Technology Today" Blast, *The Moon Over Star,* and "Star Parties" help you understand the ways technology affects us?**

COLLABORATE

Talk About It Look at the photograph and read the caption. Talk with a partner about what Claudia Mitchell is able to do with her prosthetic arm.

Cite Text Evidence Think about how technology has made Claudia's life better. **Circle** clues in the photograph that show what Claudia can do with her prosthetic arm. **Underline** evidence in the caption that shows how she controls her new arm.

Write I understand how technology affects us because the authors _____

_____

_____

_____

_____

_____

_____

Win McNamee/Getty Images News/Getty Images

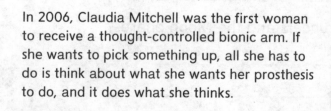

In 2006, Claudia Mitchell was the first woman to receive a thought-controlled bionic arm. If she wants to pick something up, all she has to do is think about what she wants her prosthesis to do, and it does what she thinks.

Present Your Work

COLLABORATE

Discuss how you will present your flyer about something that will improve your community. Plan to explain how the images make your multimodal brochure more effective. Use the Listening Checklist as you practice and give the presentation. Discuss the sentence starters and write your answers.

An interesting fact I learned about our community is _____

_____

_____

_____

I would like to know more about _____

_____

_____

✓ Listening Checklist

☐ Listen carefully to questions from the audience.

☐ Ask for more details if you do not understand the question.

☐ Make eye contact with the audience as you ask for feedback.

☐ Take notes as you listen to comments.

kali9/E+/Getty Images

Talk About It

Essential Question

How do writers look at success in different ways?

COLLABORATE

A baseball team winning a championship is one kind of achievement. A person petting a dog can be an achievement, too, if he or she has been afraid of dogs for a long time. In your opinion, is success always a positive thing? Why or why not?

Talk with a partner about how you define success. Then fill in the graphic organizer with words that describe success.

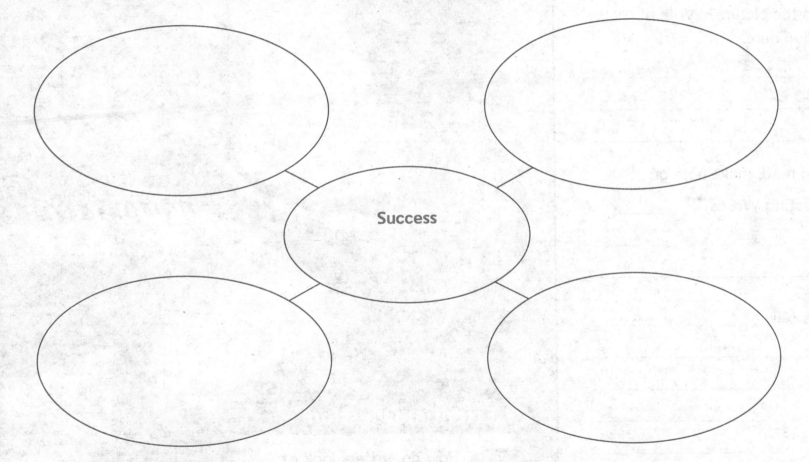

Success

BLAST BACK!
studysync

Go online to **my.mheducation.com** and read the "Defining Success" Blast. Think about the things that inspire you. Where do you find inspiration to be successful? Blast back your response.

TAKE NOTES

Read the title of the poem and look at the picture. What questions do you have about the boy in the picture? Write a question here.

_____

_____

_____

As you read, make note of:

Interesting Words _____

_____

_____

Key Details _____

_____

_____

_____

_____

_____

Sing to Me

Essential Question

How do writers look at success in different ways?

Read about how two poets share stories of success.

The cool white keys stretched for miles.
How would my hands pull
and sort through the notes,
blending them into music?

I practiced
and practiced all day.
My fingers reaching for a melody
that hung dangling,
like an apple just out of reach.

I can't do this.
I can't do this.

The day ground on,
notes leaping hopefully into the air,
hovering briefly, only to crash,
an awkward jangle, a tangle of noise
before slowly fading away.

My mom found me, forehead on the keys.
She asked, "Would you like some help?
It took months for my hands to do what I wanted."
She sat down on the bench,
her slender fingers plucking notes
from the air.

I can do this.
I can do this.

She sat with me every night that week,
working my fingers until their efforts
made the keys sing to me, too.

— Will Meyers

(bkgd) Tony Anderson/The Image Bank/Getty Images; (texture) Vincenzo Lombardo/Photographer's Choice RF/Getty Images; (tr) Mark Tomalty/Masterfile

NARRATIVE POETRY

FIND TEXT EVIDENCE 🔍

Read

Stanzas 1–4
Character

Circle the stanzas that tell how the narrator feels and sounds when playing the piano. What sentence summarizes his feelings?

_____

_____

Connotation and Denotation

Underline a word in stanza 4 with a negative connotation. Write what it means.

_____

_____

Stanzas 5–7
Theme

Draw a box around the stanza that shows the message of the poem.

Reread

Author's Craft

With a partner, discuss the lines that are the climax of the poem.

FIND TEXT EVIDENCE 🔍

Read

Stanzas 1–5

Theme

Draw a circle around what the brother says to annoy the narrator.

Draw a box around what the narrator does as she waits for the bus. What does this tell you about the narrator?

_____

_____

Connotation and Denotation

What is the connotation of the word _immense_ in stanza 1?

_____

What is its denotation?

_____

Reread

Author's Craft

How does the poet use repetition to support the theme of the poem?

_____

The Climb

"Go on, I dare you!" My brother's voice
mocking, a jaybird's repetitive screech.
We are waiting for the bus
under our immense oak tree.

I reach for the lowest branch and find
another to pull myself up before
I lose my grip on the slippery bark
and slither down the trunk. Again.

Today, at school,
I drop my milk at lunch,
take a pop quiz,
and argue with my friends.

Today is my birthday.
When I get off the bus,
The oak tree doesn't look
any smaller or bigger.

Today, I am ten years old.
I reach for the lowest branch
and find another to pull myself up.
My hands find another and another.

Over and over among the red
outstretched leaves,
foot to branch: push!
hand to branch: pull!

My brother is rooted on the ground,
staring up at me,
until finally, I can't climb any higher,
or I will be a cloud.

— Sonya Mera

Summarize

Compare how the characters in each poem feel to how you feel when you are successful.

Stanzas 6–7
Stanza and Repetition
Circle the words the poet repeats in stanza 6. What effect does the repetition have?

_____

_____

Theme
Underline the action words in stanza 6 that help set up the theme. Write the words on the lines.

_____

Reread
Author's Craft

What image does the poet use to describe the narrator's brother?

Fluency

Poetry is meant to be read aloud. Practice reading the poem aloud to a partner. Make sure you read with feeling. Discuss how reading poetry aloud is different from reading other kinds of texts.

Vocabulary

Use the example sentences to talk with a partner about each word. Then answer the questions.

attain

The mountain climber wanted to **attain** the goal of being the first person to reach the peak.

What goal would you like to attain?

_____

_____

dangling

The ripe apple was **dangling** from the end of the branch.

What are some things you might find dangling?

_____

_____

hovering

The hummingbird was **hovering** in front of the flower's petals.

Write a sentence about something you have seen hovering.

_____

_____

triumph

Winning the state championship was a **triumph**!

What is a synonym for _triumph_?

_____

Poetry Terms

stanza

A **stanza** is one or more lines of poetry that form a unit of a poem.

Explain how you know when a stanza ends.

_____

_____

repetition

Poets who repeat words or phrases in a poem are using **repetition**.

How might repetition add to a poem's meaning?

_____

_____

Connotation and Denotation

denotation

The **denotation** is the basic definition of a word. It is an example of literal language.

What is the denotation of the word *little?*

_____

_____

connotation

The **connotation** is a meaning suggested by a word in addition to its literal meaning.

What is the connotation of the words *scrawny cat?*

_____

_____

Build Your Word List Reread "Sing to Me" on page 157. Underline three words that look interesting to you. In your writer's notebook, write the three words. Use a an online or print thesaurus to find two synonyms for each word. Write a sentence using one of the synonyms for each word.

Connotation is a feeling or idea connected to a word.

Denotation is the dictionary's definition of a word.

FIND TEXT EVIDENCE

When I read "Sing to Me" on page 157, I know that some words suggest positive or negative feelings. The denotation of the word slender *is "thin." Slender* has *a positive connotation, as in "long and elegant." Slender* is very different from the word scrawny, *even though the denotation for both is "thin."*

She sat down on the bench, her slender fingers plucking notes from the air.

Your Turn Reread "The Climb" on pages 158–159. What are the definition and feeling of the word *screech?* In your writer's notebook, write the word, its denotation, and its connotation.

You can look for context clues—other words around it—to help you figure out the connotation of a word.

_____

_____

Tony Anderson/The Image Bank/Getty Images

Stanza and Repetition

A **stanza** is two or more lines of poetry that together form a unit of the poem. Stanzas can be the same length and have a rhyme scheme, or vary in length and not rhyme.

Repetition is the use of repeated words or phrases in a poem. Poets use repetition for rhythmic effect and emphasis.

🔍 FIND TEXT EVIDENCE

Reread the poem "The Climb" on pages 158–159. Identify the stanzas and listen for words and phrases that are repeated.

Quick Tip

When poets repeat words, they want you to notice specific words or ideas. When you see a repeated word or phrase, ask yourself: "What is the important idea that the poet is telling me here?"

- *The words repeated in "The Climb" are . . .*

- *The word Today begins three stanzas because . .*

Page 158

The Climb

"Go on, I dare you!" My brother's voice mocking, a jaybird's repetitive screech. We are waiting for the bus under our immense oak tree.

I reach for the lowest branch and find another to pull myself up before I lose my grip on the slippery bark and slither down the trunk. Again.

Today, at school, I drop my milk at lunch, take a pop quiz, and argue with my friends.

Today is my birthday. When I get off the bus, The oak tree doesn't look any smaller or bigger.

Today, I am ten years old. I reach for the lowest branch and find another to pull myself up. My hands find another and another.

Stanza Each of these groups of lines is a stanza.

Repetition The poet starts the last three lines on this page with "Today."

Your Turn Reread "Sing to Me" on page 157. What two lines does the poet repeat in this poem? What effect does the repetition have?

_____

_____

_____

_____

Narrative Poetry

Narrative poetry tells a story and has characters. A narrative poem

- can be about fictional or real events
- may be written in stanzas

 FIND TEXT EVIDENCE

I can tell that "Sing to Me" and "The Climb" are narrative poems because they both tell a story and have characters.

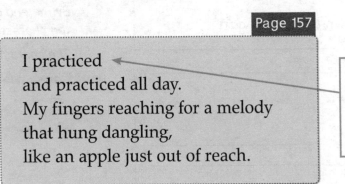

Page 157

I practiced
and practiced all day.
My fingers reaching for a melody
that hung dangling,
like an apple just out of reach.

Character
The narrator of the poem
is the main character.
We see the events from
his point of view.

Your Turn Reread the poem "The Climb" on pages 158–159. Identify the elements that tell you it is a narrative poem.

_____

_____

_____

_____

_____

Readers to Writers

Pay attention to pronouns if you are having trouble figuring out who the speaker is in a narrative poem. Pronouns like *I, me,* and *my* are clues that the narrator is telling the story in the first person. The pronoun *she* or *he* makes it a third-person point of view. In your own writing, remember to use pronouns to show your point of view.

Theme

The theme is the main message, or lesson, in a poem. Identifying key details in a poem can help you determine the theme.

🔍 FIND TEXT EVIDENCE

I'll reread "The Climb" on pages 158–159. I will look at the narrator's words and actions to help me identify the theme.

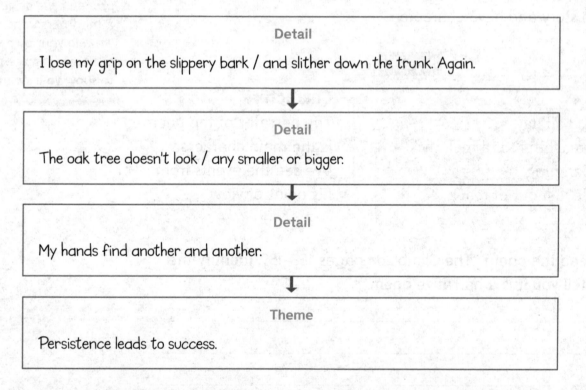

Detail
I lose my grip on the slippery bark / and slither down the trunk. Again.

⬇

Detail
The oak tree doesn't look / any smaller or bigger.

⬇

Detail
My hands find another and another.

⬇

Theme
Persistence leads to success.

Your Turn Reread "Sing to Me" on page 157. Find the key details and list them in the graphic organizer. Use the details to determine the theme of the poem.

Quick Tip

To find the theme, you can ask: "What lesson does the character learn in this poem?" or "How do the characters change from the beginning to the end of the poem?" Use these sentence starters.

- *In the beginning, the character is . . .*
- *By the end of the poem, the character is . . .*
- *The character learns . . .*

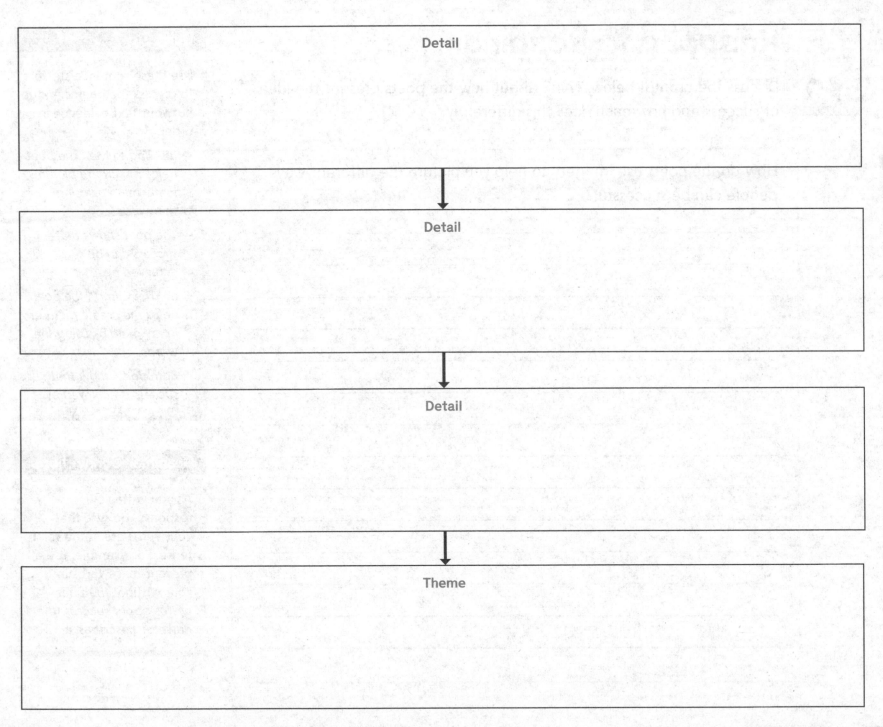

Detail

Detail

Detail

Theme

Respond to Reading

COLLABORATE

Discuss the prompt below. Think about how the poets present the idea of success and how each does this differently.

How do the poets use imagery to help you picture the different ways people can be successful?

_____

_____

_____

_____

_____

_____

_____

_____

_____

_____

_____

_____

Quick Tip

Use these sentence starters to discuss the poems and to put your text evidence in order.

- In "Sing to Me," the poet helps me create pictures in my mind by using the words . . .

- The poet shows that success can be achieved by . . .

- In "The Climb," the poet helps me create pictures in my mind by using the words . . .

- Both poets show that success is achieved by . . .

Grammar Connections

As you write your response, be sure that your verbs are in the same tense. For example, use all present-tense verbs in your writing: _the poet **writes** about success; the narrator **describes** . . ._

How to Conduct an Interview

During an **interview**, you ask a person questions about his or her life, work, and experiences. First, learn as much as you can about the person. Next, follow these steps:

- **Make contact.** Send an e-mail, write a letter, or phone the person to ask for an interview. Agree on a place and time for the interview.
- **Prepare.** Brainstorm ten questions you would like to ask. Practice asking them with a partner. Clarify any questions if they are unclear.
- **Listen.** During the interview, take notes and listen closely.
- **Review.** After the interview, review your research and your notes. Circle sections you think you will want to use later.

This student is interviewing an adult who has helped in her community. What questions do you think she might ask?

_____

_____

_____

Interview a Community Helper With your partner, think about people who have helped your community. Decide on the best person to interview by answering these questions:

- How has this person changed your community in positive ways?
- Will others be interested in hearing what this person has to say?
- Do I know somebody who could introduce me to this person?

Develop and follow your research plan with adult assistance. Share your ideas with your teacher before you begin. Discuss how you will contact the person and conduct the interview. After you finish your interview, you will present your interview to the class.

 Tech Tip

If your interviewee agrees, use a laptop, tablet, or cell phone as a recording device. With a partner, practice asking and recording your questions. Be sure to place the device where both you and the interviewee can be heard clearly.

Fuse/Getty Images

Swimming to the Rock

*Literature Anthology:
pages 310–315*

? **How does the poet help you visualize how the narrator feels as she watches her father and brothers swim?**

Talk About It Reread stanzas 3–5 on pages 310 and 311 of the **Literature Anthology**. Talk with a partner about what the narrator's father and brothers are doing.

Cite Text Evidence What words and phrases show what the narrator sees as she watches them swim? Write text evidence in the chart.

Text Evidence	Why It's Important

Write The poet helps me visualize how the narrator feels by _____

_____

_____

💡 Evaluate Information

Sensory words relate to the things we can see, hear, touch, smell, and taste. Which sense does the poet use the most words to describe? How would the poem be different if the author did not use sensory words?

The Moondust Footprint

What words and phrases does the poet use to express the mood and feeling of the narrator?

Talk About It Reread page 312. Talk with a partner about how the narrator describes the Moon landing.

Cite Text Evidence What words and phrases create mood? Write text evidence in the chart.

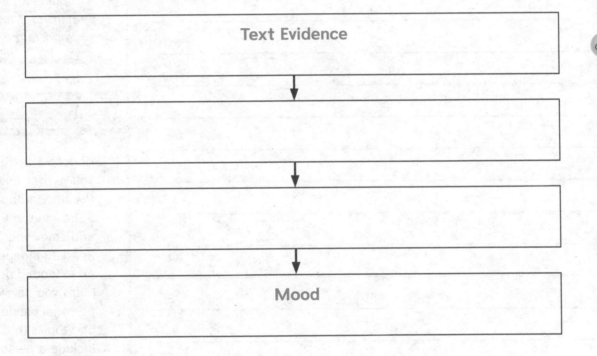

Text Evidence

↓

↓

↓

Mood

Write The poet expresses the mood and feeling of the narrator by _____

_____

_____

For a better understanding of how sensory words create a mood, use the sentence starters below.

- *During a rain storm, I see . . .*
- *The rain sounds like . . .*
- *The rain smells like . . .*
- *The rain feels . . .*

Synthesize Information

Combine what you know about repetition and sensory words and images. Think of words or phrases to express how you felt about watching an exciting event. Use sensory words to describe your mood and the event.

Respond to Reading

Discuss the prompt below, and share any questions you have with a partner. Apply your own knowledge of success to inform your answer. Use your notes and graphic organizer.

Compare and contrast the narrator's feelings in "Swimming to the Rock" and "The Moondust Footprint."

_____

_____

_____

_____

_____

_____

_____

_____

_____

_____

_____

_____

NASA

Quick Tip

Use these sentence starters to talk about and cite text evidence.

- _The poets of both poems use descriptive language to . . ._
- _This language helps me understand the narrator's feelings by . . ._
- _Understanding the narrator's feelings is important because . . ._

Self-Selected Reading

Choose a text and fill in your writer's notebook with the title, author, and genre. Set aside some time to read and enjoy your selection. Reading independently for an extended period of time helps you develop a personal connection to texts and topics that interest you. Include a personal response to the text in your writer's notebook.

Genius

 How does the poet use figurative language to help you understand what the narrator is like?

Literature Anthology: pages 314–315

 Talk About It Reread the last two stanzas on **Literature Anthology** page 314. Talk with a partner about what the narrator and his sister are doing.

Cite Text Evidence What words and phrases describe the narrator's sister? Write text evidence in the chart.

Figurative Language	What I Understand

Write The poet uses figurative language to help me understand _____

_____

_____

Quick Tip

Figurative language is used to compare two different things. Use these sentence starters to help you understand figurative language.

- *The narrator compares his sister to a . . .*

- *They are being compared because both are . . .*

Winner

 How does the poet help you understand how the narrator feels about his father?

 Talk About It Reread the last stanza on page 315 of the **Literature Anthology**. Talk with a partner about what the narrator says his dad does when he hits the ball.

Cite Text Evidence What phrases show how the narrator feels about his father? Write text evidence in the chart and tell how it helps you understand.

Text Evidence	How It Helps

Quick Tip

You can use these sentence frames to talk about the narrator's father.

- *The poet describes how the father reacts by . . .*
- *This language helps me understand that the narrator feels . . .*

Write I know how the narrator feels about his father because the poet

_____

_____

Character and Plot

A narrative poem has characters and a plot. Often the main character tells the story, using the first person. Narrative poets develop their plots with a series of events. There is usually a beginning, a middle, and an ending. In one of the events there is a rising action or climax.

FIND TEXT EVIDENCE

Reread "Genius" on page 314. Review the different events in the beginning, middle, and end of the poem. On the lines below, write how the narrator feels and thinks in each event that helps to develop the plot.

Beginning: _____

_____

Middle: _____

_____

End: _____

_____

Your Turn Reread "Winner" on page 315. What words tell you how the father feels about his son?_____

_____

_____

How would you describe the dad?_____

Quick Tip

Add dialogue in your narrative poem to show how the characters feel and think. To make sure your poem sounds natural, read your poem aloud. Use different voices for the different characters. Do the characters sound the way you picture them? If not, revise the language.

Readers to Writers

Whether they are long or short, all narrative poems have a plot, so the stories they tell have a beginning, a middle, and an end. The beginning is known as the rising action, or where the character identifies a problem. In the middle is the climax, where the story reaches a turning point. The falling action is where the problem starts to get solved. The end, when the problem is solved, is known as the resolution.

Text Connections

? Think about the "Defining Success" Blast and the poems you read this week. How does Douglas Malloch's description of success compare to the way the writer of the Blast and the other poets use words and phrases to tell what success means?

Talk About It Read the poem. Talk with a partner about how the poem describes what it means to be a success.

Cite Text Evidence **Underline** words and phrases that show how the poet describes what success means. Put **checkmarks** in the margin beside text evidence where the poet is comparing two things.

Write Douglas Malloch and the poets I read this

week describe success by _____

_____

_____

_____

_____

_____

_____

from
Be the Best of Whatever You Are

We can't all be captains, we've got to be crew,
    There's something for all of us here.
There's big work to do and there's lesser to do,
    And the task we must do is the near.

If you can't be a highway then just be a trail,
    If you can't be the sun be a star;

It isn't by size that you win or you fail—
    Be the best of whatever you are!

—by Douglas Malloch

Expression and Rate

Think about the meaning of a poem when you read aloud. Reading a poem aloud with **expression,** or feeling, makes the poem more interesting. The **rate** is the speed at which you read a poem. Commas, dashes, and other punctuation marks can tell you when to slow down, stop, or read with expression. Paying attention to the expression and rate can make the poem's meaning clearer to listeners.

Page 157

> The day ground on,
> notes leaping hopefully into the air,
> hovering briefly, only to crash,
> an awkward jangle, a tangle of noise
> before slowly fading away.

The commas in this poem signal places to pause while reading.

Your Turn Turn back to page 157.
 Take turns reading "Sing to Me" aloud with a partner. Pay attention to punctuation. Visualize what is happening in the poem. How does the poet want the reader to feel? Express your feelings in the way you read the poem.

Afterward, think about how you did. Complete these sentences.

I remembered to _____

_____

Next time I will _____

_____

McGraw-Hill Education

Expert Model

Features of Narrative Poetry

Narrative poetry tells a story in a poem. The story can be made-up or based on a real event. The lines of the poem may or may not rhyme. A narrative poem

- tells a story and has characters

- is about fictional or real events

- is usually written in stanzas

Literature Anthology: Page 312

Word Wise

On page 312, the poet uses the words *Mission Control in Houston, Apollo, Landing Module, Sea of Tranquility,* and *Neil Armstrong* to show that the poem is based on real-life events.

Analyze an Expert Model Studying narrative poems will help you learn how to write a narrative poem. **Reread** "The Moondust Footprint" on page 312 of the **Literature Anthology**. Write your answers below.

Who are the characters in the poem? What are they doing? _____

_____

_____

What stanza in the poem has a rising action or climax? _____

_____

_____

_____

Plan: Choose Your Topic

Freewrite With a partner, talk about successes and things you have achieved. Then, on a separate sheet of paper, quickly write about your achievements. Don't worry about spelling or grammar. Pick two achievements and write them below.

_____

_____

Writing Prompt Write a narrative poem about one of your achievements.

I will write about _____

Purpose and Audience An author's purpose is his or her main reason for writing. Look at the three purposes for writing below. Underline your purpose for writing a narrative poem.

to inform, or teach   to persuade, or convince   to entertain

Think about the audience for your poem. Who will read or hear it?

My audience will be _____

I will use _____ language within a realistic sequence of events when I write my poem.

Plan In your writer's notebook, make a flow chart to plot out the sequence of events in your poem. Fill in the boxes with the main events of your poem. Be sure to list the events in time order.

Quick Tip

Talking with a partner about your ideas for your poem can help you plan which events come first, next, and last. Drawing pictures of the events can also help you plan. Draw pictures next to the boxes on your chart.

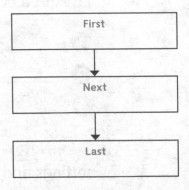

First

Next

Last

Plan: Sequence

Put Events in Order You need to plan the sequence of your poem before you begin to write. **Sequence** is the order in which key events take place. If you were writing a story, it would be easy to separate the beginning, middle, and end into paragraphs. In a poem, you can separate the beginning, middle, and end into stanzas. You can also include transition words and phrases to help the reader figure out the sequence:
At first, . . .; Then, . . .; Before long, . .; After that, . . .; Finally, . . .

To make sure you cover everything, answer these questions.

- What feelings did you have before your achievement?

- What was the first thing that happened on the way to that achievement?

- What were you seeing, hearing, and smelling while you were doing it?

- How did you feel when you finally achieved what you wanted to do?

List three events that you will write to tell about your achievement.

1 _____

2 _____

3 _____

Take Notes Once you know what your poem is about, make a list of your settings and characters. Use your flow chart to plot out the events of the story. Include only the most important details about each event to keep your chart entries brief. Use transitions to link your ideas together.

Draft

Figurative Language Poets use figurative language, such as similes and metaphors, to help readers draw pictures in their minds. A **simile** compares two unlike things using the words *like* or *as*. A **metaphor** compares two unlike things without using the words *like* or *as*.

> In the morning, I was as busy as a bee working on my collage. My hands were like scissors, cutting pieces of paper into circles, triangles, and squares.
>
> Slowly, I felt my energy starting to fade like a shooting star. By noon, I was no longer a bee but a snail.

Think about a person, a feeling, and an object that will be part of your poem. Write a simile and a metaphor for each of them.

Person simile: _____

Person metaphor: _____

Feeling simile: _____

Feeling metaphor: _____

Object simile: _____

Object metaphor: _____

Write a Draft Write the draft of your poem in your writer's notebook. Remember to use sequence words and to include similes and metaphors. Explain how the figurative language will create images in the reader's mind.

Revise

Alliteration Poets like to play with words. Alliteration is a tool they use to make language more interesting. Alliteration is the use of the same beginning consonant sound in a line. Say the following sentence aloud to see how fun alliteration can be.

> Skyler's skateboard skidded past a skittish skunk.

Read the sentences below. Then revise one or more words in each sentence so that they contain alliteration. A thesaurus can help you find the precise word you need.

Jay leaped over his coat and grabbed a drink.
Maria always baked when she was angry so she made cupcakes.
Gabby collected the trash and offered it to Gavin.

_____

_____

_____

_____

_____

Revision Revise your draft, and check that you have alliteration to make the language in your poem more interesting and fun. Also, review your similes and metaphors to make sure their meanings are clear.

Peer Conferences

COLLABORATE

Review a Draft Listen carefully as your partner reads their work aloud. Take notes about what you liked and what was difficult to follow. Next, tell what you liked about the draft. Ask questions that will help the writer think more about the writing. Offer suggestions that will make the writing stronger. Use these sentence starters.

I liked the way you described how things sounded and looked because . . .

Can you add words that show how you're feeling during this part . . . ?

I don't understand this stanza. Can you explain what . . . ?

Partner Feedback After your partner gives you feedback on your draft, write one of the suggestions that you will use in your revision. Refer to the rubric on page 183 as you give feedback.

Based on my partner's feedback, I will _____

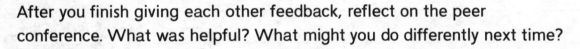

After you finish giving each other feedback, reflect on the peer conference. What was helpful? What might you do differently next time?

Revision As you revise your draft, use the Revising Checklist to help you figure out what text you may need to move, elaborate on, or delete.

> ## Digital Tools
> For more information on peer conferencing, watch the "Peer Conferencing" video. Go to **my.mheducation.com**.

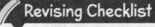

✓ Revising Checklist

- ☐ Does my poem have a beginning, middle, and end?
- ☐ Are sequence words used to help order the events?
- ☐ Did I use sensory words to help readers picture the characters and setting?
- ☐ Does the figurative language I use make sense to the reader?
- ☐ Did I include alliteration to make my poem fun and interesting?

Edit and Proofread

When you **edit** and **proofread** your writing, you look for and correct mistakes in spelling, punctuation, capitalization, and grammar. Reading through a revised draft multiple times can help you make sure you're catching any errors. Use the checklist below to edit your sentences.

✓ Editing Checklist

- ☐ Do your pronouns agree with the nouns they're referring to?
- ☐ Is there a space between the poem's stanzas?
- ☐ Are possessive nouns and contractions used correctly?
- ☐ Are quotation marks used correctly?
- ☐ Are all words spelled correctly?

List two mistakes you found as you proofread your essay.

1 _____

_____

2 _____

_____

Tech Tip

Spell checkers are useful tools in word-processing programs, but they may not recognize incorrect usage, such as *there* when you mean *they're*. Spell checkers don't replace a careful reading to find errors.

Grammar Connections

Make sure that pronouns match the noun that they refer to. For example, if you are writing about going to softball practice with friends, you should use the pronoun *we*. If you are writing about someone inviting you and your friends to the game, use the pronoun *us*.

A reflexive pronoun tells about an action that a subject does for or to itself. The ending *-self* is added for singular pronouns. The ending *-selves* is added for plural nouns. *The Queen herself will attend the event.*

Publish, Present, and Evaluate

Publishing As you prepare to **publish** your final draft, be sure to write legibly in cursive. Check that you are holding your pencil or pen correctly between your forefinger and thumb.

Presentation When you are ready to **present** your work, rehearse reading your poem aloud to a classmate. Use the Presenting Checklist to help you.

Evaluate After you publish your writing, use the rubric below to **evaluate** your writing.

What did you do successfully? _____

What needs more work? _____

_____

✓ Presenting Checklist

- ☐ Stand or sit up straight.
- ☐ Speak clearly and with expression.
- ☐ Make sure your reading rate matches the feelings you are describing.
- ☐ Gesture as you read sensory words to help listeners visualize.

4	3	2	1
• has a clear beginning, middle, and end	• has a beginning, middle, and end	• tells a story, sometimes out of sequence	• told in a disorganized or non-narrative style
• writing includes rich sensory details	• writing includes some sensory details	• writing includes few sensory details	• writing includes few to no sensory details
• figurative language is used to describe characters, feelings, and objects	• figurative language is used to describe some characters, feelings, or objects	• some use of figurative language	• very little or no use of figurative language
• few or no errors in grammar, spelling, or punctuation	• some errors in grammar, spelling, and punctuation	• frequent errors that might confuse the reader	• many errors make it difficult to follow

Spiral Review

You have learned new skills and strategies in Unit 4 that will help you read more critically. Now it is time to practice what you have learned.

- Prefixes
- Cause and Effect
- Pronunciations
- Synonyms
- Point of View
- Repetition
- Stanzas

Connect to Content

- Dust Bowl Project
- Words Related to Government
- Write a Narrative Poem

Read the selection and choose the best answer to each question.

DUST BOWL Blues

1 Have you ever seen a blizzard? All that snow blinding everything in its path? Now imagine instead of snow, heavy winds blowing tons of dust everywhere. During the Great Depression, people called these dust storms "black blizzards." In 1932, there were fourteen of them. A year later, there were almost forty. What caused these dust storms? Why did the Great Plains—including parts of Oklahoma, Texas, Kansas, Colorado, and New Mexico—become known as the "Dust Bowl"?

"It Turned My Farm Into a Pile of Sand"

2 During the 1910s and 1920s, rising wheat prices and government policies created a land boom. Homesteaders, including those in Texas, ripped up grasslands to plant wheat. As a result, there was no strong root support for holding the soil together. Grass and trees are like anchors for topsoil. By the 1930s, the depleted farms met a new foe: the worst drought in U.S. history. Most of the country was debilitated (dē-bi-lə-tā-tid). The once waving wheat fields turned to rolling dust clouds.

"Dusty Old Dust"

3   As the crops died in the over-plowed lands, the farms turned to dust. Then the storms began. Heavy winds threw tons of dust into the once blue sky, forcing everyone into complete darkness. Then just as quickly, it was half-light everywhere. Businesses and schools closed. People couldn't believe what they saw: dust as high as fences! People began wearing gauze masks to keep the sand out of their eyes, nose, and mouth. Families would place wet blankets over windows to keep out the grit.

"Dust Can't Kill Me"

4   Starting in 1935, the Great Plains began to generate new life. The Soil Conservation Service was founded in 1935 to give the Great Plains new life. It enacted farm rehabilitation (rē-ə-bi-lə-tā-shən). Farmers planted trees and changed their farming techniques. They planted trees, rotated crops, and rested the land. Through these conservation efforts, the dust settled. By 1938, dust storm numbers were reduced by more than half.

5   Finally, it rained heavily in 1939, ending the drought. By 1941, most of the destruction was repaired. But, generations across the Great Plains would never forget those Dusty Bowl days.

Dust storms would blow millions of tons of dust into the air.

© U.S. Department of Agriculture

1 According to paragraph 2, what was one of the causes of the depleted farms?

    A The grain prices were high.

    B There were rolling clouds.

    C Farmers removed the strong root support.

    D Grasses and trees are anchors for topsoil.

2 Read the following information about the origin of the word <u>enacted</u>.

> from the English prefix *en-,* meaning "to put in" +
> Latin *act,* meaning "to establish"

This information helps the reader know that the word <u>enacted</u> in paragraph 4 means —

    F ended

    G passed

    H repeated

    J answered

3 The author included "(rē-ə-bi-lə-tā-shən)" after the word <u>rehabilitation</u> because —

    A it tells the origin of the Latin roots.

    B it explains what the word means.

    C it shows how to pronounce the word.

    D it identifies a foreign vocabulary word.

Quick Tip

If you are not sure which answer is correct, try identifying answers that you know are *not* correct. Cross them out. Then choose the answer that best answers the question.

Read the selection and choose the best answer to each question.

"Flying" FREE

I flew from that poor Texan farmhouse
with thirteen mouths to feed,
and no Pa to help our Ma.
I flew from that one-room
5 wooden schoolhouse with no
paper or pencils to write with.

Fate's compass guided this Texan to Chicago
where the streets were dirty,
and the looks of discrimination, dirtier.
10 Fate's compass guided this Texan from aviation school
to aviation school,
each door locked to black women, like me.

Mon coeur, my heart, took off in France
where I learned to pilot the skies,
15   the only place free from prejudice.
Mon coeur, my heart, took off in France
where I lifted my race and gender and
prepared the way for *all* aviatrixes.

The logbook recorded my barnstorming
20   heart-thrilling stunts, loops, and turns
for spectators who would accept others like me.
The logbook will record me, Bessie Coleman,
when I crash-land, plummet, and dive—
only to eternally soar free.

1 What do all of the stanzas have in common?

  A The stanzas are all five lines long.

  B The last two lines of each stanza have rhyming words at the end.

  C The stanzas contain dialogue between the narrator and others.

  D The first and fourth lines start with repetition.

2 In stanza 3, a synonym for the words <u>took off</u> is —

  F learned

  G piloted

  H lifted

  J prepared

3 The last stanza explains that —

  A Bessie Coleman flew planes for free.

  B Bessie Coleman's logbooks were interesting to read.

  C Bessie Coleman went to France.

  D Bessie Coleman was not afraid of adventurous stunts.

4 From which point of view is the poem written?

  F first-person

  G second-person

  H third-person limited

  J third-person omniscient

Quick Tip

If you are not sure what a question is asking, reread it and underline or circle details. Then reread the text to find evidence to answer the question.

HOMOPHONES AND HOMOGRAPHS

COLLABORATE

Homophones are words that sound alike but have different meanings, origins, and spellings. **Homographs** are words that are spelled the same, but have different meanings and origins. Sometimes homographs are pronounced differently.

- Use a print or online dictionary to identify the parts of speech and meanings of the words below.

- The words *reign/rain* are homophones. The word *land* is a homograph.

rain

Part of Speech: _____

Definition: _____

reign

Part of Speech: _____

Definition: _____

land

Part of Speech: _____

Definition: _____

Part of Speech: _____

Definition: _____

Grammar Connections

Because they sound alike, it is easy to mix up homophones. When you write, be sure to use the correct spelling of any words that are homophones. Consider these examples: *ate, eight; our, hour; night, knight; right, write; sell, cell.*

Choose a pair of homophones from the examples above. Write a sentence using each word. Explain why you used that homophone in the sentence. Use a dictionary if you are not sure which word to use.

SETTING

The **setting** is the time and place in which a story takes place. Some settings take place in the present and others in the past or future.

- Reread "Dust Bowl Blues" and "Flying Free." Identify the historical settings and how they impacted the people in the passages.

Setting	How Characters Were Affected

ALLITERATION AND ASSONANCE

Alliteration is the repetition of the initial sounds in words that are near each other, such as in "The sneaky snake snickered." **Assonance** is the repetition of similar vowel sounds followed by different consonant sounds, such as the short *a* sound in "The sad captain left after he had a nap."

- Write a name for an animal using alliteration.

- Name: _____

- Write a silly sentence about the animal using assonance.

- Silly Sentence: _____

DUST BOWL PROJECT

Reread "Dust Bowl Blues." Look for one or two facts in the passage. Write questions you have about the facts. Then research the facts to find the answers to your questions.

- Select a genre that you would like to write in, such as a journal entry, a letter, or a newspaper article.

- Use your Dust Bowl research to write your text in your writer's notebook.

- Include precise language and domain-specific vocabulary.

The genre I selected to write about my topic is _____

_____

WORDS RELATED TO GOVERNMENT

Latin roots can help you figure the meanings of unfamiliar words. You can check the meanings of Latin roots in a dictionary.

- Use a print or online dictionary to find words with the base *govern*, from the Latin root *gubernare*, meaning "to govern."

- Make a word web. Write *govern* in the middle circle. Then write the new words with the definitions in the other circles.

How do people in your community participate in state government?

_____

_____

WRITE A NARRATIVE POEM

Narrative poems tell a story. They can be written from the first-, second-, or third-person point of view. Narrative poems can include characters, setting, and plot.

- Research a historical figure important to your state's history.

- Use the facts to write a narrative poem about that person.

- Compose your poem in stanzas.

- Include repetition, alliteration, assonance, or rhyming.

Write your poem here. _____

_____

_____

_____

_____

_____

_____

_____

I chose this historical figure because _____

_____

_____

WHAT DID YOU LEARN?

Use the rubric to evaluate yourself on the skills that you learned in this unit. Write your scores in the boxes below.

4	3	2	1
I can successfully identify all examples of this skill.	I can identify most examples of this skill.	I can identify a few examples of this skill.	I need to work on this skill more.

☐ Point of View   ☐ Cause and Effect   ☐ Synonyms

☐ Homophones   ☐ Latin Roots

Something that I need to work more on is _____ because

_____

_____

_____

Text to Self Think back over the texts that you have read in this unit. Choose one text and write a short paragraph explaining a personal connection that you have made to the text.

I made a personal connection to _____ because

_____

_____

_____

_____

Conduct Your Interview

Discuss how you will conduct your interview. Use the interview checklist as you practice your interview. Discuss the sentence starters below and write your answers.

An interesting fact that I learned about the person is _____

_____

_____

_____

I would like to know more about _____

_____

_____

_____

_____

_____

Quick Tip

It can be challenging to take notes while someone is talking. Consider recording the interview and taking notes later. Be sure to get permission to record.

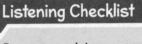

Listening Checklist

☐ Be prepared. Learn as much about the person as you can.

☐ Write your questions before the interview.

☐ Take your time with each question.

☐ Listen attentively to the responses.

☐ Take notes and get permission to record the interview.